Sandwich Bay

30
8855

12

8

11

Hades

The
Great and
Unknown
Sahara

6

The Maiden

The Corset

9

7

3

4

5

Keeper's
Cottage

2

The
Kitchen

D1401373

THE OPEN
CHAMPIONSHIP
1985

WRITERS

DAVID DAVIES
PETER DOBEREINER
JOHN HOPKINS
RAYMOND JACOBS
MICHAEL McDONNELL
DONALD STEEL
MICHAEL WILLIAMS

PHOTOGRAPHERS

LAWRENCE LEVY
BRIAN MORGAN

EDITOR

BEV NORWOOD

AUTHORISED BY THE
CHAMPIONSHIP COMMITTEE
OF THE ROYAL AND ANCIENT
GOLF CLUB OF ST. ANDREWS

THE OPEN
CHAMPIONSHIP
1985

SPRINGWOOD BOOKS
ASCOT, BERKSHIRE

© 1985 The Championship Committee Merchandising Limited

First published 1985
Springwood Books Ltd, Ascot, Berkshire

Printed in Great Britain

Statistics of 114th Open Championship
Produced on a Burroughs Computer System

All photographs taken on KODAK Ektachrome
and Kodachrome professional films

Overview photograph of eighteenth hole
by Jim Brown

Royal St George's course map
by Frank Bissette

Photographs of Henry Cotton
© Wide World Photos

Springwood Books
Ascot, Berkshire

ISBN 0 86254 126 3

CONTENTS

THE CHAMPIONSHIP COMMITTEE

G. B. B. JEFFREY, *Chairman*
G. M. SIMMERS, O.B.E., *Deputy Chairman*

J. R. BOARDMAN
W. G. BURLEIGH
A. W. DICKIE
J. P. GRANT
T. E. D. HARKER
R. D. JAMES
A. J. LOW
M. J. REECE
R. T. ROBINSON
Sir ROSS STAINTON, C.B.E.
H. THOMSON
R. YOUNG

Additional Member
E. A. C. DENHAM
Council of National Golf Unions

M. F. BONALLACK, O.B.E., *Secretary*

W. G. WILSON, *Deputy Secretary*

D. HILL, *Championship Secretary*

INTRODUCTION

By Gordon B. B. Jeffrey

Chairman of Championship Committee
Royal and Ancient Golf Club of St Andrews

The Championship Committee of the Royal and Ancient Golf Club is pleased to present its second annual to record the 114th Open Championship at Royal St George's.

Once again we owe sincere thanks to our editor and to the publishers, photographers and writers, all of whom have contributed handsomely to this lasting memento of Sandy Lyle's fine victory on the historic links which compliment the picturesque old town of Sandwich.

It has again been a memorable championship culminating in the first Open victory for a British golfer since 1969.

We hope you will enjoy reading this year's annual and that you will think it is a fitting record of Sandy Lyle's championship.

Gordon B B Jeffrey

Lots of people have asked me what it is like to acknowledge victory in this championship. I feel very much like a medical student or any other person who has passed an exam. That person was just as clever some months before the exam as he is immediately afterward. But once he has passed that exam, he is qualified — there is now a rod by which his skill may be measured. I do not think I am a better player today than I was a week before the championship but I am qualified.

Henry Cotton, 1934

FOREWORD
By Sandy Lyle

It was a dream come true to win the Open Championship, which was my ambition for a long, long time. I remember as a schoolboy sitting in the stand beside the last green at Royal Lytham when Tony Jacklin won in 1969. I just missed catching Tony's ball when he threw it into the crowd after holing the winning putt. I thought how nice it would be to play in the championship—and to win. I was golf mad, even in those days. I had a feeling I would win the Open, but I didn't know when.

The keys to my victory were undoubtedly the fourteenth and fifteenth. I hit a two iron 220 yards into the wind to the green at the fourteenth. At the fifteenth I hit a six iron to about ten or twelve feet, and holed that one as well. That was the crucial putt. I almost burst into tears, because it was so exciting to get back into contention. But I never lost control.

I wanted to make four on the eighteenth, because I thought there would be a play-off if I took five, and was trying to get the pitch between four and five feet away to give myself a chance at par. I played it delicately with a sand wedge, and it didn't pay off. The easiest thing would have been to hit it hard, five or six yards past the hole. I could easily have three-putted from there. Once my ball had rolled down the hill, all I was concentrating on was getting down in two. Fortunately I got the first putt reasonably close and made the next.

I am delighted to have this annual as a permanent record of my victory, and I hope you will also enjoy recalling those tense and exciting moments at Royal St George's.

Sandy Lyle

9

114th
OPEN CHAMPIONSHIP

★ Denotes amateurs

Name	Scores				Total	Money
Sandy Lyle, Scotland	68	71	73	70	282	£65,000
Payne Stewart, USA	70	75	70	68	283	43,000
Jose Rivero, Spain	74	72	70	68	284	23,600
Christy O'Connor Jr, Ireland	64	76	72	72	284	23,600
Mark O'Meara, USA	70	72	70	72	284	23,600
David Graham, Australia	68	71	70	75	284	23,600
Bernhard Langer, Germany	72	69	68	75	284	23,600
Anders Forsbrand, Sweden	70	76	69	70	285	15,566
D. A. Weibring, USA	69	71	74	71	285	15,566
Tom Kite, USA	73	73	67	72	285	15,566
Eamonn Darcy, Ireland	76	68	74	68	286	11,400
Gary Koch, USA	75	72	70	69	286	11,400
Jose-Maria Canizares, Spain	72	75	70	69	286	11,400
Fuzzy Zoeller, USA	69	76	70	71	286	11,400
Peter Jacobsen, USA	71	74	68	73	286	11,400
Simon Bishop, England	71	75	72	69	287	7,900
Sam Torrance, Scotland	74	74	69	70	287	7,900
Greg Norman, Australia	71	72	71	73	287	7,900
Ian Woosnam, Wales	70	71	71	75	287	7,900
Ian Baker-Finch, Australia	71	73	74	70	288	5,260
Jaime Gonzalez, Brazil	72	72	73	71	288	5,260
Lee Trevino, USA	73	76	68	71	288	5,260
Graham Marsh, Australia	71	75	69	73	288	5,260
Mark James, England	71	78	66	73	288	5,260
Philip Parkin, Wales	68	76	77	68	289	3,742
Kristen Moe, USA	70	76	73	70	289	3,742
★ Jose-Maria Olazabal, Spain	72	76	71	70	289	—
Michael Cahill, Australia	72	74	71	72	289	3,742
David Frost, South Africa	70	74	73	72	289	3,742
Gordon Brand, England	73	72	72	72	289	3,742
Manuel Pinero, Spain	71	73	72	73	289	3,742
Robert Lee, England	68	73	74	74	289	3,742
Ove Sellberg, Sweden	71	78	70	71	290	3,150
Wayne Riley, Australia	71	70	77	72	290	3,150
Hugh Baiocchi, South Africa	75	74	71	71	291	2,862
Ben Crenshaw, USA	73	75	70	73	291	2,862
Andy Bean, USA	72	72	73	74	291	2,862
Bob Shearer, Australia	75	73	68	75	291	2,862
Tony Johnstone, Zimbabwe	68	72	80	72	292	2,600
Magnus Persson, Sweden	71	73	76	72	292	2,600
Jeffrey Pinsent, England	73	74	72	73	292	2,600
Seve Ballesteros, Spain	75	74	70	73	292	2,600
Corey Pavin, USA	70	74	72	76	292	2,600
Peter Senior, Australia	70	71	80	72	293	2,400
Ronan Rafferty, N. Ireland	74	73	71	75	293	2,400
David A. Russell, England	74	72	71	76	293	2,400
Denis Watson, South Africa	72	74	75	73	294	2,128
Mark Mouland, Wales	72	75	74	73	294	2,128
Gordon Brand Jr, Scotland	69	74	77	74	294	2,128
Bernard Gallacher, Scotland	73	76	71	74	294	2,128
Howard Clark, England	70	71	76	77	294	2,128
Tom Watson, USA	72	73	72	77	294	2,128

Name	Scores				Total	Money
Nick Faldo, England	73	73	75	74	295	1,750
Emilio Rodriguez, Spain	71	70	77	77	295	1,750
Larry Nelson, USA	70	75	75	77	297	1,625
Peter Fowler, Australia	70	79	70	78	297	1,625
David Whelan, England	69	74	75	80	298	1,550
David Williams, England	74	71	74	81	300	1,500
Vaughan Somers, Australia	76	72	73	80	301	1,460
Bob Charles, New Zealand	70	76	69	Ret'd	—	1,400

Non-Qualifiers After 54 Holes

(All professionals receive £700)

Gary Player, South Africa	72	77	73	222
Steve Martin, Scotland	74	74	74	222
Terry Gale, Australia	75	73	74	222
Craig Stadler, USA	76	72	74	222
David Ray, England	73	74	75	222
★David Gilford, England	72	74	76	222
Jeff Mathews, England	74	71	77	222
Chris Moody, England	72	77	74	223
Lanny Wadkins, USA	73	74	76	223
Paul Way, England	71	76	76	223
Ossie Moore, Australia	73	73	77	223
Michael King, England	71	75	77	223
Tony Charnley, England	75	74	75	224
Bill McColl, Scotland	69	80	75	224
Eddie Polland, Ireland	72	77	75	224
Paul Thomas, Wales	75	74	75	224
Peter Teravainen, USA	73	74	77	224
Chen Tze Ming, Taiwan	74	71	79	224
Des Smyth, Ireland	75	74	76	225
Kikuo Arai, Japan	71	78	76	225
Massimo Mannelli, Italy	74	74	77	225
Paul Oglesby, USA	76	69	80	225
Manuel Ballesteros, Spain	74	75	77	226
Grant Turner, England	72	74	80	226
Ray Carrasco, USA	73	76	81	230

Non-Qualifiers After 36 Holes

(All professionals receive £375)

Ian Mosey, England	73	77	150
Woody Blackburn, USA	74	76	150
Michael Ingham, England	73	77	150
Chris Platts, England	74	76	150
Mark McNulty, South Africa	74	76	150
Mark McCumber, USA	75	75	150
Glenn Ralph, England	78	72	150
Peter Dahlberg, Sweden	73	77	150
Derrick Cooper, England	75	75	150
Simon Hobday, South Africa	72	78	150
Bob Byman, USA	72	78	150
Denis Durnian, England	75	75	150
Nick Price, South Africa	74	77	151
Carl Mason, England	75	76	151
Neil Coles, England	75	76	151
Peter Harrison, England	72	79	151
Steve Cipa, England	76	75	151
John Bland, South Africa	73	78	151

Michael Clayton, Australia	72	79	151
Shinsaku Maeda, Japan	75	77	152
Jamie Howell, USA	75	77	152
Jack Nicklaus, USA	77	75	152
Krister Kinell, Sweden	76	76	152
Tommy Horton, England	76	76	152
Tateo Ozaki, Japan	76	77	153
Rodger Davis, Australia	75	78	153
Rick Hartmann, USA	76	77	153
David Llewellyn, Wales	74	79	153
David Armstrong, Australia	71	82	153
Eduardo Romero, Argentina	74	79	153
Bill Bergin, USA	73	81	154
Gary Smith, England	74	80	154
Tony Jacklin, England	81	73	154
Alan Tapie, USA	79	75	154
Nick Godin, England	75	80	155
Brian Sharrock, England	79	76	155
★Jonathan Evans, Australia	79	76	155
Ken Brown, Scotland	72	83	155
Bill Longmuir, Scotland	76	79	155
Brad Faxon, USA	75	80	155
Vicente Fernandez, Argentina	76	79	155
Clive Tucker, England	78	78	156
Brian Marchbank, Scotland	76	80	156
Baldovino Dassu, Italy	78	78	156
Lee Jones, England	77	79	156
★Mark Davis, England	78	78	156
★Garth McGimpsey, N. Ireland	78	78	156
Noel Ratcliffe, Australia	77	79	156
Bill Rogers, USA	74	83	157
Michael McLean, England	72	85	157
★Graham Homewood, England	80	78	158
Jerry Anderson, Canada	79	79	158
James Heggarty, N. Ireland	77	81	158
Stephen Bennett, England	77	81	158
Christopher Bassett, England	75	84	159
Art Russell, USA	77	82	159
Naomichi Ozaki, Japan	82	77	159
Roger Chapman, England	74	85	159
Philip Walton, Ireland	74	85	159
Toru Nakamura, Japan	76	84	160
Bobby Mitchell, England	78	82	160
Maurice Bembridge, England	83	78	161
Armando Saavedra, Argentina	80	81	161
Garry Cullen, Kenya	78	84	162
Jeff Hall, England	78	86	164
★Robert Purdie, England	77	87	164
★Richard Latham, England	84	84	168

ROUND ROYAL ST GEORGE'S

No. 1 445 Yards Par 4 As difficult an opening hole as any in championship golf. The "Kitchen" is the valley into which the drive should be dispatched but the emphasis is always on the second shot. This must be carried over two guardian bunkers and then stopped in double quick time once it pitches if a birdie putt is to be established. The best line for the drive is down the right but the rough on the right is fierce.

No. 2 376 Yards Par 4 Like so many seaside holes, varies according to the wind. In normal circumstances, the carry over the dominant bunker is not formidable with modern equipment. The longer hitters can cut off more than just the bunker although the fairway is full of humps and hollows. The safe line from the tee is to the right but the second shot from here stands more chance of breaking right down a sharp bank.

No. 3 214 Yards Par 3 This new short hole which replaced the old blind tee shot to a punchbowl green was slightly revised for the 1985 Open. There are now no bunkers but with rough engulfing the left-hand side, there are those who may wish that there were!

No. 4 470 Yards Par 4 The first real reminder of the importance of good driving at Royal St George's. Few bunkers in the world are more awesome than the one to be carried or skirted here but those deciding on the latter plan of action won't find much elbow room. Unless you hit a long drive down the right, you don't get a sight of a green which has a most distinctive and severe ridge. Out of bounds beyond the green.

No. 5 422 Yards Par 4 A definite decision to be taken about the tee shot. With a head wind, the decision is easy; simply batter it as hard as you can with a driver but, downwind or no wind, the options are greater. The idea is to set up a position on the plateau that enables you to to see the flag between the dunes which are a further feature of this left-hand dogleg.

No. 6 156 Yards Par 3 The famous "Maiden" but nothing like as formidable looking as in her youth. One of the few to grow prettier with age. From the grandstand perch on the top of the giant hill, it is possible to visualise the extent of the old tee shot from a different direction but now it looks down on a pleasant short hole where the main difficulty can be gauging the wind.

No. 7 529 Yards Par 5 In a wind from Ramsgate, can be a terrifying drive even for the world's best. A newish tee has stretched the carry over the large central bunkers to around 200 yards. The ground then dips down and the fairway angles to the left parallel to the shore. The first par five, but no limit if the drive or second shot strays.

No. 8 415 Yards Par 4 To introduce more balance between the two nines, the hole which Frank Pennink turned from a par three into a 415-yard par four against the prevailing wind. The best drives finish on the elevated part of the fairway and the best seconds reach an undulating green but there is a wide band of cross scrub and hollows short of the green to punish anything underhit.

No. 9 387 Yards Par 4 If Royal St George's demands fine driving, the shape, angling and contouring of the greens is unusually marked. The ninth is a case in point with a large slope running down from the bunkers on the left and a deep gulley awaiting anything pushed. From the left of the fairway, it is difficult to attack a pin positioned at the back left of the green.

No. 10 399 Yards Par 4 A new back tee for the 1985 Open but not the most difficult of drives. The real difficulty lies in judging the second shot to an elevated, exposed green. The landing areas are few. Walter Hagen used to play just short of the green on the upslope for fear of going over the back which is never advisable. Not quite so fearsome with modern wedges.

No. 11 216 Yards Par 3 A slightly revised green from the days when the hole was a short par four makes the target for a long par three. The tee is situated on the other side of the ridge that used to be a feature of the drive. A well bunkered green but the holing out putts are deceptive.

No. 12 362 Yards Par 4 A hole where competitors in the Open would look for a birdie but a better hole when it needs a solid drive to make the carry between the two bunkers. There are plenty of uneven stances on the fairway which bends to the right and a plethora of bunkers further on but the second shot is not too demanding. A favourite hole with the members with the refreshment hut beside the green.

No. 13 443 Yards Par 4 Another drive where you cannot see the ball finish on the fairway but a fine hole forming the beginning of Sandwich's celebrated finish.

The second shot is aimed towards the clubhouse at Prince's, scene of Gene Sarazen's Open triumph in 1932. A new bunker on the left of the green has restricted the entrance more than in 1981 but the green is just as devilish with its central spine dividing it into two.

No. 14 508 Yards Par 5 Out of bounds threatens the drive for the first and only time on the second and last of the par fives—and a very real threat it is, too. No semi-rough. Just the fairway and then the fence by Prince's. A little sculpting of the dunes has allowed a sight of the fairway denied in earlier times but the second famous feature is the stream crossing the fairway at right angles known as the Suez Canal. A birdie hole but plenty of sixes and sevens as well.

No. 15 467 Yards Par 4 One of the classic holes in golf. The drive must avoid bunkers on either side but it is the second shot which adds the spice. To be successful, it must carry a series of cross bunkers in front of a green which has a severe bank on the left and a sharp slope away to the right. It needs a bold decision and pinpoint accuracy particularly when the greens are hard and fast.

No. 16 165 Yards Par 3 Requires a headwind to bring out the best in it, a formidable short hole in the days of hickory. Large bunkers and fairly heavy mounding make the island green look smaller than it is but not difficult if it is only a mid or short iron.

No. 17 425 Yards Par 4 Another drive where position is all important but it is the second shot which can be a considerable problem. The plateau green is raised three or four feet and is much wider than it is deep. A fairly flat approach makes underclubbing a distinct possibility; in which case, you have to be certain whether to pitch or pitch and run. Many a short putt missed, too.

No. 18 458 Yards Par 4 A marvellous finishing hole, a fact not so apparent in 1981 when Bill Rogers came to the last hole with strokes in hand. The ideal drive is down the left in order to negotiate the bunker eating into the green on the right. Anything further right is in "dead man's" country, a fact that brings the slope on the left of the green more into play. It is known as "Duncan's Hollow" after George Duncan who failed to get down in two from it to tie Walter Hagen in 1922 but countless hundreds have since kept him company.

THE VENUE
Where Some Find 'Perfect Bliss'

By Donald Steel

In one sense, it is a little surprising that Royal St George's, stronghold of English golf and bearer of the name of the patron saint, was founded by two Scotsmen. In another sense, it is no more than you would expect. There is hardly a country in the world where Scottish influence was not responsible for the introduction of the game and, if that does not exactly prove beyond doubt that it was the Scots and not the Dutch who invented golf, the Scots were certainly more active in spreading the gospel.

The discovery of Sandwich, however, was far from accidental. Even in the 1880's, there was talk that London courses were becoming over-crowded. This applied principally to the commons at Wimbledon and Blackheath, the two centres of renown, although the complaint may have owed as much to the fact that there was nothing particularly attractive about the few other places round the capital where the game had taken a hold.

In one condemning sentence, Bernard Darwin later categorised some of them as being "villainously muddy in winter, of an impossible and adamantine hardness in summer and just endurable in spring and autumn." Being more precise about one in particular, he attributed it the accolade, "never by the wildest stretch of the imagination could it be called anything but a bad course." They typified the feeling of "golf in fields" but it wasn't entirely the discontent of facing long queues on first tees that stirred Dr. Laidlaw Purves, a leading opthalmic surgeon at Guy's Hospital, and Henry Lamb into action.

It was their longing to find a true links that proved the greater driving force. Like all self-respecting Scotsmen, they couldn't reconcile themselves to accepting that inland golf was anything other than a poor second to St Andrews, Prestwick, North Berwick, Dornoch or Troon. This was perhaps little wonder, but their exhaustive search for a seaside base was, at times, unavailing. They must have been on the verge of despair when they finally stumbled on their promised land alongside Sandwich Bay.

They had started at Poole, working east along the south coast where, apart from overlooking the merits of Rye, their judgement in continuing could not be faulted. In the end, they found what they were looking for in the wild duneland between the quaint, picturesque town of Sandwich and the sea. Purves, so the story goes, first "spied the land with a golfer's eye" from the top of the Norman church tower of St Clements — whither he may have gone to offer up a prayer. More important, the Earl of Guilford was ready to lease 300 acres, a company was formed, the course laid out and a dream born.

For the record, some form of golf had been played there earlier than 1887. In the 1860s, a Scottish schoolmaster named Ogilvie attempted to interest his pupils in golf, one assumes without success because, by 1870, Mr. Luck, the coast-guard, had cut five holes which he lined with gillipots in the area near the present fifth green but he was thwarted by a posting to Brancaster.

Whether he did the same there, is not known.

Anyway, Purves and Lamb, stalwarts of Wimbledon, were the guiding forces and a glance at the picture gallery of captains in the long corridor of the clubhouse, showing two of the occupants of the office dressed in kilts, emphasises how the Scottish influence lingered. It was a powerful influence, too, because those early years brought more rapid recognition for a new club than almost any other. Within seven years of its opening, Sandwich had housed England's first Open Championship (1894) and produced the first Open victory by an English professional, J.H. Taylor.

That was regarded as the signal of acclaim and, to quote Darwin again, "for some time, it would have ranked only a degree below blasphemy to have hinted at any imperfection in Sandwich." However, there gradually arose intermittent cries that all was not well but, oddly enough, it was two other Scotsmen who led the chorus of criticism.

Freddie Tait's assertion that it was a "one-shot course" was supported by Ted Blackwell, beaten finalist in the 1904 Amateur Championship to Walter Travis, the player who, described as a little man with a black cigar and a centre-shafted putter, began the fashion of American winners in Britain. Tait, a celebrated soldier in the Black Watch, chose his overwhelming victory in the Amateur of 1896 to give vent to his feelings; and quite a stir he caused.

There were no Press interviews in those days but, if there had been, one cannot help feeling there would have been some juicy pickings. The nature of his objection was the distance of the carries from many of the tees as well as the blindness of some of them. It was felt that golf should not consist of hitting shots over sandhills and then running up to the top of them to see where the ball finished, although it is hard to see why Blackwell should have been one to complain. He was said to hit the ball "malignantly hard."

Even if Prestwick had (still has) its share of blind shots, their second point was more easily understandable; indeed, before Sandwich was restored as an Open Championship venue in 1981, a number of blind shots disappeared. The old version of the third and eleventh were replaced. Part of the sand dune was moved to allow sight of the fourteenth fairway and a little more is now seen of the drives at the fourth and seventh but, in an age when driving is not always the true art it should be, Sandwich today is one of the most demanding courses in the world. But it is far more besides. Nowhere is there a richer variety of second shots.

Nevertheless, in the light of all the controversy,

it is a wonder that Royal St George's, as it became in 1902, maintained its place on the championship rota. The fact that it did can be attributed very largely to Darwin, whose passionate love of the course was no doubt of comfort to officials. Darwin considered it "nearly my idea of heaven as is to be attained on any earthly links."

"Confound their politics," Darwin once observed about the course reformers. "Frustrate their knavish tricks," he went on. "Why do they want to alter this adorable place? I know they are perfectly right, and I have even agreed with them that this is a blind shot or that an indefensibly bad hole, but what does it all matter? It is perfect bliss."

No publicity machine could have done more than Darwin did but, whatever voices were raised in anguish, they were not entirely supported by events.

Whereas Taylor won the Open in 1894 with the highest seventy-two-hole aggregate (326), Jack White of Sunningdale lowered it to 296 in 1904. He was the first winner to return a round under 70, a feat not equalled until Bobby Jones in 1927. The first winner to have two rounds under 70 was Henry Cotton in 1934, also at Sandwich.

Part of the reason for White's amazing burst of scoring (80, 75, 72, 69) lay in the advent of the Haskell ball whose benefit was undoubtedly felt more at Sandwich than anywhere. In the days of the gutty, several of the carries were formidable, not least the Maiden where players on the famous short hole, unlike today, were separated from the green by a high hill. It took a brave, strong player to "fly the Maiden" successfully but it soon needed a player with the full range of shots to play the entire course. It is no coincidence therefore that Harry Vardon won two of his six Open victories at Sandwich.

The first in 1899 was by the convincing margin of five strokes, the second in 1911 after a play-off with Arnaud Massy, Massy eventually capitulating and conceding, muttering "I cannot play zis' damn game." In the event of a tie in 1985, a five-hole play-off would have been implemented for the first time but, in spite of what the critics might say, Sandwich has been infallible in the quality of the champions it has produced.

In addition to Taylor, Vardon and White, Walter Hagen, the first American-born champion, won twice. Henry Cotton created history there in 1934 with his scoring as well as ending a spell of ten years of overseas dominance. Reg Whitcombe "reaped a whirlwind" in 1938, and before Sandwich was closed for alteration, so to speak, Bobby Locke added his distinguished name to the list. When it re-opened for business in 1981, Bill Rogers created something of a surprise, but he won by four strokes in spite of being one of the four winners in the last sixty-five years to have withstood a seven in his final round.

Then, most recently of all, Sandy Lyle, a golfer from the cradle, had the most agonising of waits before knowing that, like Cotton, he had held the overseas invaders at bay. His victory marked the end of sixteen years without a British winner and, for this reason, if nothing else, it will always be remembered.

Cotton's repulsion of all-comers in 1934 was achieved with a level of scoring that introduced a whole new dimension. His total of 132 (67, 65) for the first two rounds has never been equalled and it is worth recording that the course in use was only about 150 yards shorter than that in 1985. When you consider how greatly the manufacture of balls and equipment has advanced, you get some idea of Cotton's colossal achievement. Cotton's four-round total was 283.

Cotton's attitude to the game and to life had a lot in common with Hagen, who won again in 1928, the year Cotton finished equal eighteenth in his second Open, having been ninth the previous year. The impact of Hagen's victory and the presentation of the trophy by the Prince of Wales were events which inspired Cotton, who remains the only British golfer to have won the Open more than once since World War I. Similarly, Lyle was spectating as a lad of eleven at Lytham when Tony Jacklin won in 1969, an experience which made up his mind about life as a professional golfer.

Sandwich did a lot for Cotton, who was very much in evidence in 1985, happy for Lyle and no doubt marvelling at the way the scene has changed in over half a century. There have been marked changes, in fact, even since 1949 when Locke insisted that fresh holes be cut for the play-off with Harry Bradshaw, who later caused the Rules of Golf to be amended after finding his ball inside a broken bottle.

It wasn't a daily routine to change the holes in those days any more than there was talk about pin positions or yardage charts. Those who knew the head greenkeeper could guess at the likely spots he would choose but one aspect that has seen far less change is the problem of hotel accommodation. With so many more people requiring beds, it is a headache wherever the Open pitches camp.

As soon as Sandwich was adopted almost a hundred years ago, there were grumblings among some professionals that they had to find digs as far away as Deal and queue for a train or bus to take them to Sandwich. Nowadays, the rooms available may not be as modern as most would want but the fleet of courtesy cars has, at least, eased the

travel burdens. The loss of the Guilford Hotel, a familiar landmark from the third and fourth holes, was a blow to those wishing to see the Open return to the south-east, but Sandwich's salvation that brought an end to its Open exile lay in the construction of the long awaited by-pass.

The ancient streets of the town, which has had a port since Roman times, have never looked to me exactly ideal for a carriage and pair or penny farthing let alone a juggernaut, and its narrow, wooden toll bridge always seems to produce a bottleneck even on a quiet market day. Re-routing traffic to the by-pass was like loosening the noose from a guilty man's neck but the sceptics were still not content.

They continued to argue that it would take hours to reach the course during an Open and that, if cars got in, they would never get out again. Such gloomy prognostications affected the attendance in 1981, but there wasn't a grain of truth in the rumours. Thanks to a carefully thought out battle plan, and the exemplary help of the Kent police, Sandwich proved to be the most accessible of all our Open courses, deservedly earning another chance within four years. After some teething troubles on the first two days in 1985, everything was smoothness again, for the last two, although the crowds were vastly bigger than 1981, an overall increase of about 30,000.

The only accidental blemish on the part of the club which produced four captains of the Royal and Ancient between 1964 and 1973 is that Bobby Jones never played an Open there but he did the next best thing by helping the Americans to a resounding victory in the Walker Cup in Jones' historic summer of 1930. His defeat by 9 and 8 of Roger Wethered, his opponent in the Amateur final, was just a tasty aperitif.

Twenty-nine years later, Jack Nicklaus scored his first stroke-play victory in Britain by taking the St George's Grand Challenge Cup the week before the Amateur Championship which was won by Deane Beman, now Commissioner of the U.S. PGA Tour. Nicklaus' victory was a rather happier reminder of Sandwich than his first round of the 1981 Open when he had an 83 on an afternoon when, admittedly, the weather deteriorated, or his failure to make the last day for the first time in even more unfriendly conditions in 1985.

However, nothing could match the vileness of 1938 when conditions on the final day were described by Henry Longhurst as the worst he ever saw. In ferocious gales, Reg Whitcombe was one of only three players to break 80 twice. Alf Padgham drove the old eleventh (380 yards) downwind, holing the putt for a two and Cotton, who won in wet weather at Carnoustie the previous year, drove the second green after lunch. The rest of the scene was one of devastation, as collapsed tents resembled giant schooners that had run aground, their contents swept away like dust across the links towards Prince's.

Years before, on the eve of a championship, Arnaud Massy expressed the hope that the wind would blow so hard that it would remove every tree on the course. Either he wasn't too familiar with the topography of Sandwich or his wish was granted for, apart from a screen of trees around the clubhouse, a converted farmhouse, there isn't a tree to be seen.

It is easy to appreciate therefore that golfers at Sandwich can be colder, wetter and more miserable than anywhere else — easier still to appreciate perhaps after 1985 — but equally there can be a peace and serenity that transcends all else. Away from the turmoil of an Open, its cheering crowds and scaffold stands, there is an appealing sense of escape. The holes wind about in great dells and hollows with an occasional glimpse of the sea and only an occasional glimpse of other players.

Lark song can be the only intrusion on solitude, although rounding the great sandhills, there may be visions to be had of Taylor, Vardon or Hagen. They are the heroes who have embellished the story of Sandwich which took shape in the minds of men in London long ago but, to lesser mortals, the memory of a round on a heavenly day is even more indellible.

Few would argue with Darwin that it is "perfect bliss," least of all Sandy Lyle, whose victory would unquestionably have won a nod of approval from Laidlaw Purves and made him perform the opposite of turning in his grave. It has taken Sandwich a long time to produce a Scottish champion but it makes the founders' pioneering efforts even more appropriate and worthwhile.

Dr. Laidlaw Purves "spied the land with a golfer's eye" from the tower of Sandwich Church

Royal St. George's Clubhouse

Starter's Hut

Suez Canal on the fourteenth hole

Henry Cotton on the day of his 65 and at this year's Open

. . . putting for his third Open title

. . . driving in 1977 at Turnberry

RETROSPECTIVE
Henry Cotton, The Anti-Hero

By Peter Dobereiner

Royal St George's has provided the stage for many players to take an heroic stride along the rocky path to immortality. Open champions include J.H. Taylor, Bobby Locke and Walter Hagen (twice). Among the amateurs, John Ball, Harold Hilton, Freddie Tate and Walter Travis trailed clouds of championship glory across the links. The youthful Jack Nicklaus gave notice of his glittering future by winning the Challenge Cup and Bobby Jones, who could do no wrong in 1930, did no wrong in the Walker Cup match. And it was here four years later that a worthy recruit to this illustrious company, Henry Cotton, set out to become a legend.

Up to 1934 Cotton's record in the Open Championship had been disappointing to home fans, hungry for a British champion to end the American domination. From 1925 onwards he had failed to qualify only once but each year something thwarted his challenge. Either his putting, always the suspect part of his game, let him down, or he contracted flu, or sprained his wrist or, as in 1933 at St Andrews when he shared the lead after three rounds, he was assailed by a mood of pessimism that convinced him this was just not to be his year.

Cotton's arrival at Royal St George's was hardly propitious. He had practiced hard all year for this one event but now that the moment had arrived he was in a state of dithering despair. He had brought four sets of clubs with him and could not hit the ball properly with any of them. He even considered withdrawing from the championship for his cause was hopeless. However, on the grounds that since

he was there he might as well give it a go, he took a day off without so much as touching a club or giving a thought to golf, an unprecedented move for the dedicated Cotton, and resolved simply to turn up for the qualifying round and see what happened.

What in fact happened was that he played a virtually perfect round, 66 without benefit of fancy putting. In the first round proper he opened with 67 and followed it with the famous 65 which was to be celebrated over the next half century on successive generations of Dunlop golf balls. His aggregate of 132 for the first thirty-six holes is a record to this day.

On the last day — two rounds in those times so that the professionals could be back at their clubs for the week-end duties — he had 72 in the morning which increased his lead to nine strokes. All he had to do was stand up in the afternoon to win by a bundle, or so popular speculation had it.

Cotton reported to the tee and was informed by the starter that the time had been put back fifteen minutes for purposes of gallery control. In order to avoid the glad-handers and back-slappers congratulating him prematurely on a foregone conclusion, Cotton sat in the starter's hut. That was a mistake. His hopes and forebodings churned alarmingly in his mind and it was all too much for his delicate constitution. When he was called to the tee he could hardly stand for stomach cramps, he felt weak and his forehead was beaded with cold sweat.

His long game was pitiful and only a refreshing touch with the putter contained his score to an outward 40. He started back five, five, five and was headed for the kind of collapse which can destroy a golfer for life. Another five looked decidedly on the cards at the thirteenth but now came the key stroke which kept him on the track of his illustrious career.

It was, in truth, only a ten-footer to save par but it transformed Cotton. The terror and the tension fell from him and he played crisp, par golf from then on for 79 which gave him a winning and record-equalling total of 283.

Cotton was not a professional of the traditional, ex-caddie school. His father, George Cotton, was a modestly prosperous iron founder in Holmes Chapel, Cheshire, and when Henry was an infant the business was sold and the family moved to Dulwich. Henry and his brother Leslie were enrolled at Alleyn's school, where his main sporting interest was cricket and his ambitions were centred on a career in civil engineering. He was thus embarked on the conventional middle class track of public school, university, professional qualifications and a comfortable career with cricket and golf as recreational and strictly amateur pursuits.

Then came the incident which shattered that ordered destiny. At the end of an away match, the prefects of the Alleyn's XI ordered the plebs of the team to return to the school with the cricket gear. Henry did not take kindly to the chore of humping the bags across London on trams and trains, and posted a note that the prefects should do their share of the chores. For this mutinous act he was ordered a prefect's caning. Henry refused to be caned. The sports master decreed that Cotton could not play cricket until he submitted to his punishment and asked him: "What will you do now, Cotton minor?" Henry replied: "In that case, I will play golf."

Thus was born Henry Cotton, the anti-hero. It was a role for which he was well fitted by his rebellious nature. Although he had a natural charm, he was arrogant, self-opinionated and ruthlessly committed to the proposition that he must be his own man and do things his own way.

He turned pro at sixteen and eventually was appointed full professional at Langley Park, Beckenham. There were not many tournaments in those days and Cotton played at every possible opportunity. He was making good progress but he was always conscious that his success and his reputation were purely domestic; his ambition demanded that he must test himself against the dominant Americans.

He booked himself a first class berth on the *Aquitania* (we can add style to charm as major strands in Cotton's character) and scraped together £300 for an onslaught on the United States. In strictly financial terms the tour was not a success.

He merely broke even on the trip but in professional terms his visit was a vital element in his education as a golfer.

At this time he had a rather stilted, upright swing which produced a controlled fade. Using his hickory clubs he could not really compete against the power play of the best Americans with their new, steel-shafted clubs. Cotton was an avaricious pupil, taking full advantage of the freely offered advice of the friendly American players such as Tommy Armour and Sam Snead. He remodelled his swing, switching to a flatter arc which gave him a drawing shape to his drives and yards of extra distance. He returned home a better and wiser golfer, ready to command his place in the 1929 Ryder Cup team.

Cotton was constantly at loggerheads with his fellow professionals in the PGA, most of whom considered him to be conceited and stand-offish. They had a point because Cotton, following the lead given by the American Walter Hagen, refused to be forced into the mould of the typical pro who was content to be excluded from the clubhouse and generally treated as a servant.

Between them Hagen and Cotton elevated professional golf from a trade to a profession but their ostentatious life style earned them few friends at the time. In Cotton's case the antagonism meant that he was excluded from the next three Ryder Cup teams.

It seemed to Cotton that since he was not becoming a prophet of even making much profit in his own country it would be an astute professional move to establish himself overseas. He took the pro's job at Royal Waterloo, near Brussels, and in 1930 he was invited to tour Argentina with Aubrey Boomer, a trip which was ultimately to add the final element to his apprenticeship for greatness. When he arrived at the Mar del Plata club he discovered that a wealthy young heiress had booked a course of fifty lessons with him. It was a case of antipathy at first sight. He told her brusquely that she would never make a golfer. Maria Isabel found him insufferable. Six years later they were married and their union founded a formidable sporting partnership.

In "Toots," as she was universally known, he found a personality in which ambition, determination and courage more than matched his own. In her case these forces were allied to a fiery Latin temperament which exploded at the slightest provocation. No wife was ever more loyal or more jealous of her husband's reputation. From officious dignitaries to churlish menials, all felt the sting of her lashing fists and rapier tongue. When Cotton publicly criticised his losing Ryder Cup team as captain at Wentworth the newspapers made a big thing of his remarks and Toots tore down the newspaper bills, belabouring the hapless newsagents with her umbrella.

Wildly extravagant, wildly generous, Toots was both the reason why Cotton had to be successful and the inspiration of his success. The tensions of tournament golf played hell with Cotton's sensitive nature, producing severe problems with the stomach ulcers which were eventually to cause him to be invalided out of the R.A.F. But with Toots following him every step of every important round he never flinched and never settled for the easy option. He did not dare. They enjoyed a turbulent, blissful marriage until she died on Christmas Day, 1982.

Walter Hagen sagely observed that, given the luck, anybody can win a championship once. The real mark of a champion was to win twice. Cotton passed that test in 1937 at Carnoustie with what many observers considered to be the finest performance of his life. This time the entire American Ryder Cup team was in the field, and so it was a genuine world championship, with no reservations about the British Open champion being merely champion of the British.

This was no runaway victory. Cotton considers that in the first three rounds he did not play outstandingly better than any other competitors, as he had in the early stages at Royal St George's, but in the final round it was a different story.

He set out in an unrelenting downpour, with the greens water logged and the hollows turning into impromptu water hazards. The conditions were so hostile that distinguished players such as Denny Shute, Walter Hagen and Henry Picard, cream of the American Ryder Cup team, all scored in the eighties.

Cotton's control of his ball, his nerves and, above all, his courage was absolute. His firm putting method was just right for the saturated greens. For sound strategic reasons, he deliberately played for a five at the last hole, instead of risking the out-of-bounds with a full blooded two-iron at the flag. He aimed right and found the bunker, chipping from the hard packed wet sand with his niblick and taking two putts for a 72.

The war robbed Cotton of his prime years as a golfer, and who knows how his record might read now if he had been able to continue without interruption. In his case, therefore, we have to apply a subjective judgment to his prowess in attempting to place him in any pecking order of the giants of the game. Henry Longhurst, who was as well qualified as anyone to reach an expert conclusion, wrote that he simply could not imagine anybody hitting

the ball better than Cotton at his best.

By 1948 Cotton was getting on for a competitive athlete. Post war austerity deprived him of the food he felt he needed to get fully fit. Cotton had been fastidious about his diet, or faddy as the rest of us might put it, ever since he developed stomach ulcers as a youth through neglecting regular and balanced meals. He was always too busy practising to eat anything more than a hurried sandwich, if that, and he paid for this neglect.

He therefore decided to take advantage of kind American friends and go to the United States to build up his strength and his game before the 1948 Open. It may have been all in his mind but that is where you need it in golf and he returned full of confidence after his course of sunshine and unrationed steaks.

Muirfield's tight fairways and punishing rough suited his tidy game to a nicety. King George VI followed him in the second round and Cotton produced a right royal 66 for the occasion which set him up for a comfortable five-stroke victory, the final seal on a career unmatched among British golfers of the modern era.

Taxation drove the Cottons abroad. He designed three courses for Penina, on Portugal's Algarve coast, drawing on all his imagination and experience to convert a water-logged paddy field into one of Europe's most demanding and beautiful championship courses.

Friends and pilgrims arrived to play with the Master, or to have the acutest eye in golf diagnose their faults and exorcise them with his highly individual teaching methods. While serving Baluga caviar and French champagne at £65 a bottle to his friends, Cotton complained that he was financially strapped. His villa and five servants had to go and the Cottons moved into a penthouse suite in the hotel. That way they were saved the embarrassment of having to serve Portuguese champagne.

In July 1984 the Professional Golfers' Association gave a grand dinner for Cotton to celebrate the fiftieth anniversary of his first Open, not to mention his contribution as a prolific author, course designer, teacher and generous benefactor to young professionals. It was fitting that the PGA should honour him with a dinner, rather than simply the presentation of a memento, because good food has always been, as he claims, one of the secrets of his success. As he tells aspiring champions: "Never skimp on your meals; it is not an expense but an investment."

FIRST ROUND RESULTS

Hole	1	2	3	4	5	6	7	8	9	10	11	12	13	14	15	16	17	18	Total
Par	4	4	3	4	4	3	5	4	4	4	3	4	4	5	4	3	4	4	Total
Christy O'Connor Jr	5	3	4	3	3	2	4	3	3	3	3	3	5	5	5	3	3	4	−64
David Graham	4	4	4	4	4	3	4	4	4	5	3	3	4	5	3	2	4	4	−68
Sandy Lyle	5	4	3	4	3	3	4	4	4	5	3	3	3	5	4	3	4	4	−68
Philip Parkin	3	4	2	4	3	3	5	4	4	4	3	3	3	6	4	4	4	5	−68
Tony Johnstone	4	4	3	5	4	2	3	4	3	4	3	4	4	5	4	3	4	5	−68
Robert Lee	4	3	3	4	3	3	4	5	5	3	2	4	5	5	4	3	4	4	−68
David Whelan	4	4	4	4	3	2	5	4	4	3	3	4	4	5	5	3	4	4	−69
Bill McColl	4	4	2	3	4	3	4	5	3	6	3	4	4	4	5	2	4	5	−69
Gordon Brand Jr	4	4	3	4	4	3	5	4	4	4	2	3	4	5	4	3	5	4	−69
D. A. Weibring	4	4	4	4	4	2	6	4	3	4	3	4	4	5	5	3	3	3	−69
Fuzzy Zoeller	4	3	3	4	4	3	4	4	4	3	3	4	5	5	4	3	4	5	−69

HOLE SUMMARY

Hole	Par	Eagles	Birdies	Pars	Bogeys	Higher	Rank	Average
1	4	0	9	86	55	3	5	4.34
2	4	0	26	111	13	3	17	3.95
3	3	0	16	89	47	1	7	3.22
4	4	0	9	70	60	14	1	4.54
5	4	0	21	109	22	1	16	4.02
6	3	0	20	102	30	1	14	3.08
7	5	6	73	62	12	0	18	4.52
8	4	0	8	74	56	15	2	4.52
9	4	0	23	94	30	6	13	4.12
Out	35	6	205	797	325	44		36.31
10	4	0	22	82	45	4	10	4.20
11	3	0	9	102	39	3	6	3.24
12	4	0	18	101	29	5	12	4.14
13	4	0	10	95	43	5	8	4.29
14	5	0	25	90	24	14	11	5.24
15	4	0	7	83	55	8	4	4.43
16	3	0	24	102	26	1	15	3.03
17	4	0	9	99	40	5	9	4.27
18	4	0	8	64	75	6	2	4.52
In	3	0	132	818	376	51		37.36
Total	70	6	337	1615	701	95		73.67

Players Below Par	11
Players At Par	12
Players Above Par	130

LOW SCORES

Low First Nine	Christy O'Connor Jr	30
Low Second Nine	David Graham	33
	Emilio Rodriguez	33
Low Round	Christy O'Connor Jr	64

THE FIRST DAY
Young Christy Has A Record Start

By Michael Williams

On the eve of the 114th Open Championship Henry Cotton, now seventy-eight, had received a framed portrait from the Dunlop company commemorating one of the most celebrated rounds in the championship's long history. It was his 65 on the second day in 1934. This followed an opening 67 and it established a lead he was never to relinquish in an equally famous victory.

After ten years of American domination in which both Walter Hagen (1924-28-29) and Bobby Jones (1926-27-30) had each won the cherished silver claret jug on three occasions and Jim Barnes (1925), Tommy Armour (1931), Gene Sarazen (1932) and Densmore Shute (1933) each captured it once, it was Cotton who had at last repelled the invaders.

To commemorate that second round Dunlop struck their "65" ball, and it was not until 1977 when the Open was played at Turnberry and the American, Mark Hayes, had a 63 in the second round that the championship record was lowered.

Cotton's 65 nevertheless stood as the record at Royal St George's and while he was making his appropriate speech of thanks, his sharp mind as alert as ever, a lesser known Irishman, Christy O'Connor Jr , was changing for dinner in his hotel a few miles away.

O'Connor, though now thirty-six, is still known as "Junior" to differentiate him from his illustrious uncle, Christy Senior, who is very possibly the most famous golfer ever to have emerged from the Emerald Isle. He is known among the Irish simply as "Himself" —which has never exactly made life

easy for his nephew, since comparisons have inevitably been drawn.

O'Connor Junior has nevertheless always enjoyed life to the full, even if it has been spent mostly in a golfing shadow. He played for Britain in the 1975 Ryder Cup, the year in which he also won the Irish Open as well as tieing for the Martini International. In 1976 and 1978 he assisted another Irishman, Eamonn Darcy, in taking the old Sumrie better-ball tournament, and in 1974 he was Zambian Open champion.

But it was not until now, a comfortable looking figure with a waistline that is beginning to overhang his belt, grey hair protruding almost at right angles from beneath a squarely set white cap, that young Christy claimed worldwide attention. His opening round of 64 beat Cotton's Sandwich record by a stroke and set other landmarks, too.

Beginning at the fourth hole, which was to prove the second most difficult on the course throughout the championship, O'Connor had seven consecutive birdies. In that run he had a two (at the sixth) and a four (at the seventh). The rest were all threes. As O'Connor then proceeded to get a par three at the eleventh, followed by a birdie three at the twelfth, he played nine successive holes in 27 strokes and that was another record.

Furthermore O'Connor's opening round of 64 gave him a four-stroke lead and that equalled the record on the first day, first set by James Braid in 1908, and then equalled by Bobby Jones in 1927 and Cotton in 1934. Curiously for a golfer in such form,

O'Connor's round contained as many bogeys as it did pars (four each) and two bogeys were in the first three holes, where he took three putts each time.

However, this was to be very much the pattern of the championship, for not one player throughout the four days came off the course without at least one bogey. The man who got closest to it was Corey Pavin, of America, at the very end of this first day. He had accumulated sixteen pars and a birdie in seventeen holes but finished with a five at the last, which was to prove the hardest hole of all.

O'Connor was fortunate in that his round was completed before some steady and depressing rain moved in towards tea time. Most of those who scored inside the stern par of 70 had morning tee-off times. The five on 68 were Tony Johnstone, of Zimbabwe, David Graham, of Australia, and then three more British players in Robert Lee, Sandy Lyle and Philip Parkin.

Another five were on 69. They were Fuzzy Zoeller, the 1984 American Open champion, D. A. Weibring, who is also from the States, and another three Britons in David Whelan, Billy McColl and Gordon Brand Jr.

Among those to equal par were more Americans in Larry Nelson, the 1983 U.S. Open champion, Payne Stewart, Mark O'Meara, Kristen Moe and of course Pavin. Bob Charles, the left-handed New Zealander who won this championship as long ago as 1963, matched it, too, as did two more Britons in Howard Clark and Ian Woosnam. Altogether twelve players were on par, the others being the Australians, Peter Fowler and Peter Senior, the Swede, Anders Forsbrand, and the South African, David Frost.

The American entry was not as big as it has been sometimes in the past but Tom Watson, who was seeking a record-equalling sixth championship, launched himself safely enough with a 72. Ben Crenshaw, Tom Kite and Lee Trevino could all do no better than 73 but Jack Nicklaus, accorded not for the first time a late afternoon tee-off, caught the very worst of the weather and took 77, which was at least better than the 83 he had in the opening round on the same course four years earlier.

Beforehand all the betting was on Severiano Ballesteros, the holder, and Bernhard Langer, who had twice been runner-up (in 1981 and 1984) and earlier in the year had won the Masters at Augusta. Ballesteros, caught like Nicklaus in the eye of the storm, had a 75 but Langer did rather better with a 72.

It was nevertheless O'Connor who stole everyone else's thunder and his outward half of 30 was the same as he had done at Royal Birkdale in 1976.

Then however he had faded rather with 39 home. This time he was much more persevering. After that uncertain beginning, with three putts at the first from twelve yards or so and then another three from just short of the putting surface at the third, his putter responded as it had never done before. In his next nine holes he had no less than seven single putts, the longest being from twenty-five feet at the sixth and the shortest from two feet at the ninth.

Among the hardest tasks in such a sustained spell is keeping up the concentration, forgetting the last hole and getting on with the next. O'Connor surprised even himself with his almost blinkered approach and he was equally delighted by the manner in which he kept fading his irons to the flags.

But there almost had to be an end to it all and it came at the thirteenth, where O'Connor missed the green with an eight iron and just failed to retrieve his par. Another shot slipped away at the fifteenth, where he again missed the green and on the left and wrong side, there being little chance from there of turning three shots into two. Still, another good putt found its mark for a three at the seventeenth, and he stayed at six under par with a fine four at the last.

A man who takes at least three months off each winter, most of which is spent shooting, O'Connor has often found that his best form arrives at about the time of the Open. He could not, he thought, really have played much better, much of it being set up by solid and accurate driving.

If anybody looked likely to get near O'Connor, it was Parkin, an ebullient young Welshman who a year ago at St Andrews played in his first event as a professional, finished in level par and earned enough money to become a fully qualified tournament player in the space of four days.

Parkin certainly seems to be among the players of the future, but he could hardly believe his own eyes as he came off the thirteenth green at five under par. He knew he was not playing as well as that but he had holed from six feet for a three at the first, from twenty feet for a two at the third, from thirty-five feet for a three at the fifth, come out of a bunker and holed the putt at the twelfth and then chipped in for a birdie at the thirteenth.

Excitement and perhaps even the law of averages then began to catch up on him. Parkin started "coming over the top" and was not by any means the first to fall foul of the fourteenth. Already Peter Jacobsen, who had been cruising along very nicely at four under par, had taken a nine at this par five. He had lost his first ball in the long grass on the left, gone back to drive another and hit it out of bounds on to nearby Prince's.

Parkin did neither but he did hook to put himself in deep trouble and it was enough to make him take six. Then at the sixteenth he was bunkered from the tee, while at the last he hit his drive no more than 140 yards left and low and that was a five and a third dropped shot.

Graham, on the other hand, played the inward half (33) better than he had done the outward half (35) and this was fine golf by the Australian, who will always be remembered for the quite flawless round he played to win the U.S. Open at Merion in 1981. His 67 then, as he missed only one fairway but found every green, was right in the class of Ben Hogan or Jack Nicklaus at their absolute peak.

A most deliberate, almost mechanical golfer, Graham has never quite done himself justice in the British Open and this 68 he rated as by a long way his best performance. He knew he was fortunate to have played in the morning but his birdies at the twelfth, fifteenth and sixteenth holes, over a stretch of the course that was too much for so many, was outstanding.

Inevitably there were bogeys and one of them came at the fourth, a hole over which there had been much controversy beforehand. A new tee to the right of the old championship tee meant a carry of more than 200 yards over the steep bunker set in the side of a towering sandhill, and both Ballesteros and Nicklaus had declared the hole unreasonably difficult.

The Royal and Ancient only took action on learning that Ballesteros had twice in practice needed a drive and one iron to reach the green. He is one of the longer hitters and those not so blessed were struggling. Consequently the rough beyond the bunker was scalped to fairway level and, in a south-east wind, it was decided to use a forward tee, thirty yards or so in front. As it happened this was used only in the third round.

Graham, anyway, did not get home in two and he did hit a poor drive at the tenth, which cost him another shot. Otherwise he was delighted, enjoying not only the course but also greens that he described as being of "nice easy speed and not treacherous at all."

As sixteen years had elapsed since last a British player had won the Open — Tony Jacklin at Royal Lytham in 1969 — it was seen as a perhaps hopeful sign when Lyle, one of the home country's main contenders, came in with a 68. His form of recent weeks had been mixed with a "no return" as he headed for a 90 in the Irish Open, an 80 in the final round of the preceding Lawrence Batley tournament, but a whole cluster of sub-par rounds in between.

Lyle had said beforehand that this was the sort of course on which he felt comfortable for it demands a lot of long irons and they are among his strengths. He was also, according to his caddie, David Musgrove, driving better than he has ever done with a club acquired from Eamonn Darcy only a month or so earlier.

Lyle thought his 68 was just about the worst he could have done for he had missed five putts of around six feet and another of no more than eighteen inches at the first, which certainly got him off on the wrong foot. He had hit a nine iron just through the green, chipped neatly back and then let the tiddler get away. A 66 would certainly have been more reflective of his general play.

While Lyle missed the odd fairway, he escaped the worst of the rough and the only shot he dropped, apart from that at the first, came at the tenth, where he was short with his wedge. He would have done better to hit a nine iron. His birdies came at the fifth, seventh (with two putts), twelfth and thirteenth and none of those pleased him better than that at the thirteenth.

It had been a costly hole to Lyle in the past. Once, in the PGA Championship, he had been going along very nicely when his drive hit a mobile television camera half way down the fairway and rebounded at such a tangent that he never saw his ball again. It was therefore a hole that owed him something. Significantly Lyle played the last eight holes in two under par and he had even halves of 34.

Lee's 68 came in a continuing surge of good form that all began in the Irish Open a month or so before. He had finished eleventh and followed it with fourth place in the Monte Carlo Open, where he had a first round of 61, ninth in the French Open and twelfth in the Lawrence Batley. A former England youth international, he was playing in the Open for the first time, though this was his third season as a professional. He took to the stage quite naturally and after seven holes was three under par. Two bogeys followed but he answered those with "back-to-back" birdies and though a bunker cost him a five at the thirteenth, he finished stoutly and, like Lyle, was out and back in 34.

Johnstone, winner of the Portuguese Open at the end of the previous season, had an eagle three at the seventh in his 68. This proved to be the easiest hole in relation to par throughout the championship, mostly being downwind and Johnstone, a painstaking player, was home with a three-wood second before holing out from five yards or so. With a two at the Maiden, the sixth, and then a three at the ninth, this was a profitable little run, particularly for someone who seldom settles easily to links golf.

When Ballesteros, the pre-championship favourite after successive victories in his previous two tournaments, the Irish Open and the French Open, began with a perfect birdie three, it looked for all the world as if he was "off and running." Instead he lost both his rhythm and his putting touch when he had to await a ruling at the fourth, where his chip to the green was marginally blocked by a scoreboard. Why Ballesteros thought a ruling was even necessary is another matter and the R & A firmly dismissed his claim that he had to kick his heels for twenty-five minutes.

Nonetheless, it led to a run of six bogeys in the space of eight holes—interrupted admittedly by a birdie at the seventh where he was home in two with a four iron—and by then the rains had set in. Normally Ballesteros is as good a bad weather player as anyone but on this occasion both the elements and the course got to him. Three bogeys in a row from the twelfth all added up to a 75, which he described as "not a very nice round at all."

Nicklaus admits to not being a good "rain player." Indeed, he hates it. Consequently it was the last straw after his 3.20 starting time, which was about the same hour that he had gone off four years ago. The weather closed in as he was playing the seventh and at once he got an unkind kick off the fairway at the eighth. An even more unkind lie led to a six and with three putts at the ninth, he was out in 39.

It is not easy to make up lost ground over Royal St George's exacting inward half, particularly in the wind and rain, and Nicklaus fell another victim of the fourteenth hole as he drove out of bounds. No doubt he envied Watson's morning tee off time but this other multiple champion did not perform much better than the season's form had suggested.

Nevertheless, it might have been worse, for Watson began with a six. He drove into the rough, hacked clear and then thinned his little pitch through the green. One of those strokes was retrieved at the seventh, but at the fourteenth he again yielded to par, hitting his second from the rough into the Suez canal and taking six. So a 72 it was but overall he was far from unhappy with it.

Langer was on the same mark, making much lighter of the weather than Ballesteros did, even though they were out within twenty minutes of one another and the belief in many minds that this could be the West German's year was in no way diminished.

Christy O'Connor Jr. was four strokes
ahead with his 64

The first tee at the start of the 114th Open
Championship

In pursuit of O'Connor were David Graham (next page), Tony Johnstone (top left), Robert Lee (top right), Sandy Lyle (bottom left) and Philip Parkin (bottom right)

Five-times champion Tom Watson (72)

Defending champion Seve Ballesteros (75)

Greg Norman (71)

Peter Jacobsen (71)

Manuel Pinero (71)

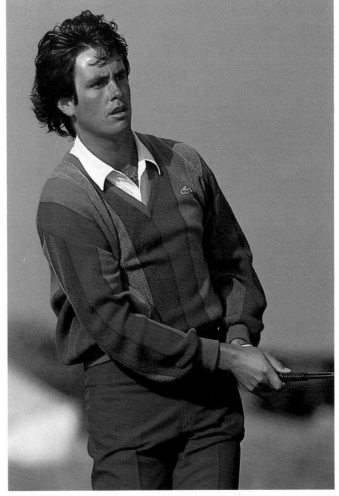

Nick Faldo (73)

Ian Baker-Finch (71)

COMMENTARY
'Junior' Escapes The Shadow

By Raymond Jacobs

The vision of the stage Irishman, like that of his Scottish counterpart, has mercifully died out in proportion to the diminishing number of stages on which those travesties could be performed. The charicatures portrayed in the likes of *Finigan's Rainbow* and *Brigadoon* have, as was once said in another time and in another context, "been utterly cryit downe and not to be uset." And yet old habits do die hard and the image of the golfing Irishman persists.

Depending upon the age of the uncommitted observer the swing, the style, the method — call it what he might — of the Irish golfer has always been a matter for wonder. No-one to witness at first hand the flailing genius of James Bruen, the bell-ringer's grip of Harry Bradshaw or the slashing attack of Joe Carr could fail to acknowledge with gratitude the innocent abandon of the Irish approach to the game. The Irish play golf as obliquely as they use language.

Christy O'Connor Sr, though, was not out of the native mould. To be sure, his swing had a marvellous, instinctive flow and, as an improvisor of shots, few of his generation of professionals were fit to touch the hem of his double-knits. But there was, to those who enjoyed watching an anarchic approach to golf, a disorderly element of the orthodox in the O'Connor swing. Had, they asked incredulously, the Irish started to worry and learned to embrace the dull virtues of conformity?

Certainly, there remained Eamonn Darcy's undisciplined right elbow and Ronan Rafferty's unbuttoned assault on the ball to uphold the established Irish verities. More worrying, however, were the apparently well-tutored swings of John O'Leary, David Feherty, and Des Smyth. What was the off-shore island golfing race coming to when grip, stance, and method more closely resembled strict allegiance to a military training manual than an unfettered licence to search and destroy? Reassurance was, happily, at hand.

Christy O'Connor Jr is no libertarian when he wields the club; his treatment of the ball is of the short, sharp shock variety. But there remains a pleasing sense of individuality in his three-quarter swing, which delivers a punch-like blow that is in complete contrast to the fluent flamboyance that has been his celebrated uncle's bench-mark. Junior's judicious attack once gained him first place in the season's statistics as Europe's most accurate driver — a flagrant contravention of everything that Irish waywardness holds dear.

Deny the contention and retreat from it as he might, O'Connor's tournament career struggled to prosper under the long shadow cast by Senior's exploits. Junior's countrymen asserted that he profited less than he should have done by winning — and what else? —the 1975 Irish Open. Less aggressive and more approachable than his uncle, he was said to have no sooner stepped from under Senior's stifling reputation than to have stepped back beneath it again — and not ungratefully at that.

But O'Connor Junior was still able to make a name for himself long before he shook the golfing world with his epochal score of 64. His driving, by contemporary standards, may have been a little short, his long iron play less than piercing, and his putting not of the most assertive. To his compatriots, though, O'Connor has been something of a valued adviser when questions of course management, the strategy and tactics of the game, have arisen.

O'Connor was said, too, to lack aggression, to enjoy the life-style of the PGA European Tour without applying himself in the way all who would succeed, and sustain success, must do. Somehow, the very fact that O'Connor was an accordion player and singer of more than average ability reinforced the opinion that however admirable these talents might be, and even if they offered a legitimate release from the grind of the tournament existence, no golfing good could come of them.

Never mind O'Connor's modest placings in the Order of Merit in previous seasons, his performances leading up to this Open Championship were, with one appropriately coincidental exception, so intrinsically nondescript as to take everyone totally unawares when he unleashed his historic score on the first day. As this Irishman jigged the rest, by comparison, reeled.

Four weeks before the Open O'Connor, on no less a course than the one inescapably associated with his uncle—Royal Dublin—had finished equal eighth in the Irish Open. In nine other tournaments his placings ranged from nineteenth to seventy-fifth. When O'Connor arrived at Royal St George's he was forty-first on the Order of Merit table, with £10,629; when he left he was eleventh and his earnings had more than trebled to £34,229.

How, therefore, to account for a transformation that seemed as unlikely an achievement as catching lightning in a bottle? Those of a romantic, even nationalistic, disposition might attribute it to a certain extent to what might be described as O'Connor's pride of place. Improbably for a touring professional, he and his family live in Gort, near Galway in the remote West of Ireland, in a house built on land formerly owned by the renowned Lady Gregory.

This formidable personality was a notable patron of the arts in Ireland — associated especially with the Abbey Theatre in Dublin and the poet W.B. Yeats. What that connection has to do with a card that bettered by one stroke Henry Cotton's well-nigh legendary 65 in the second round of the Open at St George's fifty-one years before; equalled Craig Stadler's 64 in 1983 at Royal Birkdale as the lowest opening score in 114 championships, and included a record for the Open of seven successive

birdies appears, superficially, inconsequential.

But only the devout agnostic would deny the influence of what one sportswriter of long ago, wise in the ways of the unforeseen, described as "the incalculable factor"— that coalescing of an individual performance within a team effort, a weakness previously undetected but conditioned by the pressures of the occasion, a co-ordination of the mind and body so resplendent that the athlete might truly be said to be in "a state of grace."

Golf being the game it is adds other factors to the equation. There is the bounce of the ball, not always away from the hole. There is the starting time, when good or bad weather will have a critical influence on a score. There are the pairings, in which compatability between players and their pace of play can be of importance. Clear eyes, firm wrists, steady knees, a settled digestion, and no doubt, rising on the right side of the bed also help.

Frequently, too, a new club, or a variation of an old one, will act as a placebo. O'Connor's accuracy from the tee was thoroughly established; now approaching thirty-seven, the age when a tournament professional's career has, in seasonal terms, reached autumn, he needed the encouragement of distance. His driver of five weeks was an adaptation of one he had used for seven years; the swingweight an apparently ponderous D7, but lightened by the attachment to an uncommonly heavy head of a graphite shaft.

O'Connor came into the championship having played well enough over the previous three months without being rewarded as fully as he felt he might have been. This state of his play was not unfamiliar to him, for he customarily takes three months off during the winter, so that it is mid-summer before his game begins to come together. Three hard-working practice rounds convinced O'Connor that he was as well prepared as he could reasonably expect.

How well did not immediately become clear. Once before, in the 1976 Open Championship at Royal Birkdale, O'Connor reached the turn in 30, but in the end could do no better than 69. There was no indication that O'Connor would go out in that same figure when he took three putts from thirty-five feet at the first. A wedge shot to twelve feet at the second retrieved that bogey, whereupon O'Connor gave the stroke back with three putts from the bottom shelf of the third green.

Who knows what inspires a professional to exceptional feats of low scoring? Adequate form, of course; unimpaired concentration, too. The feeling that he can do no wrong; the run of the ball. A reservoir of fearlessness as well, which allows a player the rare luxury of becoming excited by what he is achieving yet insulates him from the kind of emotional instability that will undermine the construction of his score.

For instance, Johnny Miller, who won the Open in the same year that O'Connor first went out in 30, had a well-documented reputation for the capacity to close his mind to everything but the hole being played — forgetting what had happened before, ignoring what was yet to come. Miller once had six successive birdies in the Masters at Augusta and he made nine birdies in the final round of 63 which won him the U.S. Open title in 1963 at Oakmont. O'Connor, though, surely cut a less likely bravura figure.

Whereas Miller was the blond, lissome college type, O'Connor's silver hair bursts from beneath a white cap set in place with regimental rectitude and his silhouette more closely resembles the proportions of an apprentice alderman than a finely-honed athlete. Luckily, golf is a game which agreeably accommodates to every known build and degree of fitness, a truism which O'Connor set about confirming with as irreverent an assault on a venerable links as could be imagined.

Maintaining concentration has never been easy for O'Connor, but on this occasion he succeeded in shutting out distractions and playing each hole in its proper isolation. Afterwards, apart from the obvious pleasure he was entitled to take from the score itself, he derived special satisfaction from having sustained a disciplined frame of mind. He also was pleased with the fade he put on his iron shots, making the ball stop that much more quickly on the receptive and comfortably-paced greens.

O'Connor's putter did the rest. The ball fairly flowed into the hole from all angles and ranges, wonderfully enlivening the grey and cheerless weather which until then had made totally incomprehensible Bernard Darwin's description of St

George's: "This is perfect bliss...as nearly my idea of heaven as is to be attained on any earthly links." It would have been much more understandable for O'Connor himself to adopt that view of the course, even on a day when it looked far from its best and played little short of its most awkward.

When it was all over O'Connor's comment on the way his score improved inexorably resembled the emotions of a man in the throes of experiencing first love: "I did not know when it was going to stop and I hoped it wouldn't." Bogeys at the thirteenth and fifteenth holes did break the spell before the flourish of a final birdie, his tenth, at the seventeenth hole. Once again, though, the psychological barrier had been raised, preventing a more extreme form of excess, such as breaking 60.

Yet one ghost had been laid to rest, if only temporarily—that of Christy Senior, who, his many other exploits apart, had been runner-up in the Open once, third twice, and in the first six seven times. Twice before Junior had been the leading domestic professional in the championship, no mean achievement, but one appearance in the Ryder Cup match to Senior's ten and two tournament victories to more than twenty by his uncle represented harsh comparisons between the substance of their respective careers.

At first, indeed, it had been difficult for O'Connor to live with his uncle's name and reputation, which stood almost as rebukes when he was supposed to have failed to live up to them. Later it was recognised that he did not have his uncle's ability and he was quite happy with that judgement, for he had his own way to make in the golfing world. For one day Christy Junior did succeed in stepping out from Senior's shadow, but his more creditable achievement still in not going instantly into reverse thrust, the direction taken by so many journeymen leaders after the first round of the Open Championship, meant that O'Connor's unaccustomed place under this sun was not eclipsed.

SECOND ROUND RESULTS

Hole	1	2	3	4	5	6	7	8	9	10	11	12	13	14	15	16	17	18	Total	
Par	4	4	3	4	4	3	5	4	4	4	3	4	4	5	4	3	4	4		
David Graham	4	3	3	4	4	3	5	4	5	5	3	4	4	5	4	2	5	4	−71	−139
Sandy Lyle	6	4	4	4	4	2	4	4	3	4	3	4	4	6	4	3	4	4	−71	−139
Christy O'Connor Jr	5	4	4	5	3	3	6	5	5	4	3	4	5	6	4	2	4	4	−76	−140
D. A. Weibring	4	4	3	5	4	3	5	4	4	5	4	4	3	4	4	3	4	4	−71	−140
Tony Johnstone	4	4	3	5	5	4	4	4	4	4	3	4	3	5	4	3	4	5	−72	−140
Peter Senior	4	4	2	4	4	3	4	4	4	4	3	4	5	4	5	2	7	4	−71	−141
Robert Lee	4	4	3	4	4	3	4	5	4	4	4	5	5	5	5	2	4	5	−73	−141
Bernhard Langer	4	3	3	4	4	3	4	5	4	4	3	4	4	4	3	4	4	5	−69	−141
Howard Clark	3	4	3	5	5	3	3	4	4	4	3	3	4	5	6	3	4	5	−71	−141
Emilio Rodriguez	4	5	3	5	4	3	4	4	4	4	2	4	4	6	4	2	4	4	−70	−141
Ian Woosnam	4	4	3	6	3	3	5	4	4	4	2	4	4	5	4	3	4	5	−71	−141
Wayne Riley	5	4	2	4	4	3	5	3	3	5	3	3	5	5	4	3	4	5	−70	−141

HOLE SUMMARY

Hole	Par	Eagles	Birdies	Pars	Bogeys	Higher	Rank	Average
1	4	0	6	87	55	5	8	4.39
2	4	1	25	105	22	0	17	3.97
3	3	0	10	84	54	5	6	3.35
4	4	0	4	41	72	36	1	5.00
5	4	0	12	113	26	2	16	4.12
6	3	0	12	94	41	6	9	3.27
7	5	6	66	75	6	0	18	4.53
8	4	0	5	62	68	18	3	4.69
9	4	0	12	87	45	9	10	4.34
Out	35	7	152	748	389	81		37.66
10	4	0	11	78	49	15	7	4.46
11	3	0	22	91	35	5	13	3.15
12	4	0	14	99	35	5	13	4.20
13	4	0	12	96	40	5	11	4.25
14	5	0	20	83	39	11	12	5.28
15	4	0	12	71	54	16	5	4.51
16	3	0	15	107	27	4	15	3.13
17	4	0	1	72	70	10	4	4.59
18	4	0	1	50	86	16	2	4.77
In	35	0	108	747	435	87		38.34
Total	70	7	260	1495	824	168		76.00

LOW SCORES

Low First Nine	Eamonn Darcy	32
	David Williams	32
Low Second Nine	Terry Gale	34
	Steve Martin	34
	Jeff Mathews	34
	Larry Nelson	34
	Mark O'Meara	34
	Emilio Rodriguez	34
	Bob Shearer	34
	Alan Tapie	34
Low Round	Eamonn Darcy	68

Players Below Par	3
Players At Par	2
Players Above Par	148

THE SECOND DAY
A Test Of Skill And Patience

By Michael Williams

July may be one of England's summer months, but it does not always behave like it. This was such a day, until mid afternoon anyway when the sun at last began to break through. But from first light until well after lunch, low grey cloud scudded across the flat Kent landscape from the rough direction of Canterbury, the wind moaned among the dunes and grandstands and with it came rain.

Sandwich is a bleak and inhospitable place at such times. For some it would remind them of a May day in 1975 when Arnold Palmer, his face stung by wind and rain, his hands like vice on the club, won the PGA Championship on this same links with an heroic last round of 71. For some it would remind them of Palmer at Royal Birkdale in 1961, as he battled through the elements to build a platform for his first Open Championship victory.

For others, with longer memory, it would remind them of Royal St George's in 1938, when Reg Whitcombe won the Open with a last round of 78; more than one player needed four drivers to reach the green at the fourteenth; the English amateur champion, Frank Pennink, incurred six penalty strokes on the greens as his ball kept moving after he had addressed it, and the exhibition marquee was blown to smithereens.

The wind was not of such strength on this second day of the championship but it was enough to make the game a test of supreme skill, endurance and patience. Yet such ultimately was the difference in conditions that whereas in the morning Seve Ballesteros could not reach the seventeenth green with two wooden club shots, Sandy Lyle, in a by now gentle evening, played the same hole with a drive and "three-quarter nine iron."

Golf never has been, and probably never was intended to be, a fair game but there is no doubt that those out in the afternoon of the first day and in the morning of the second got the rough end of the draw. Yet one of them, Bernhard Langer, played what had to rank as probably the finest round of the championship when, in the very worst possible weather, he got round in 69 for a total of 141 and set a target only those out later in the day managed to pass.

Nonetheless, when opportunity beckons, the chance must be taken and at the end of this second round, the half-way point in the championship, it was Sandy Lyle and David Graham, of Australia, who share the lead on 139. Both had 71s, Lyle overcoming a potentially disastrous start when he took six at the first and then a four at the short third.

It meant that in no time at all they had overhauled Christy O'Connor Jr who, by comparison to the ten birdies he had had in his first round of 64, now ran up seven bogeys in his first fourteen holes on his way to a 76. This left him sharing third place, a stroke behind the two leaders, alongside Tony Johnstone, of Zimbabwe, and D.A. Weibring, an American who had qualified for the Open via a high finish in the Batley tournament a week earlier. Johnstone took 72 and Weibring 71.

Langer came next in a group of seven. They included three British players in Ian Woosnam (71),

Robert Lee (73) and Howard Clark (71) and were on the same mark, as was one of the lesser known Spaniards, Emilio Rodriguez.

American involvement was somewhat limited at this point but Mark O'Meara, who had been enjoying a fine season in the States, was well placed on 142 after a second round of 72; Greg Norman, of Australia, was just one shot behind him and then came another large group including the Americans, Andy Bean and Corey Pavin.

Even Tom Watson (72, 73) was not yet out of it, but Ballesteros almost certainly was. He barely qualified for the last two rounds, scores of 75, 74 leaving him on the extreme limit. If there was some relief in that, for no championship likes to see one of its favourite sons departing the scene before its final act, this was also a day of sadness. For the first time in his career, all the way back to 1962 indeed, Jack Nicklaus missed the cut.

Caught, as he had been late on Thursday, by the weather, Nicklaus had a forlorn look about him, almost as if he was asking himself what he was doing here. He had made no secret that Royal St George's was his least favourite course on the Open Championship rota, though whimsically he also claimed that this did not mean he disliked it. But a 75 on top of a 77 was three strokes too many, and he bade his farewell to the championship not, as he has so often done in the past, in the Press interview tent but sitting on a bench in the locker room.

There was a suspicion in some quarters that Nicklaus might choose to declare this as his last Open. He quickly refuted any such idea. Already he was looking forward, he said to Turnberry in 1986, by which time he would be more completely recovered from the cartilage operation he had some months before. It had prevented him from squatting on his haunches as he lined up putts. Instead he had to half crouch, like most golfers of senior status.

But the familiar wave was still there as Nicklaus, in his yellow waterproofs like some coxswain from the Deal lifeboat, came up the eighteenth fairway. His three Open Championship victories, the seven times he has been runner-up and three occasions on which he has been third in twenty-three years will always be remembered with affection and gratitude.

Meanwhile, another generation was on the march and high among them, or so it seemed, was Langer, who had brought with him to England his guru, Willi Hofmann, coach, adviser and wise counsellor. Hofmann must have been well pleased with his charge for Langer mastered the severe conditions of wind and rain like the Master golfer he had become a few months earlier.

Langer concentrated on keeping his rhythm as best he could. He tried not to rush his shots, but the most difficult task lay in club selection. At the eighth, for instance, he hit two drivers and was still short of the green. This was the first stroke he dropped to par, though he was still out in 34, having picked up birdies at the second and long seventh, where a six iron was ample with which to reach the green.

So far so good, and an almost breathtaking round was in prospect when, after five more consecutive pars, Langer made birdies at both the fourteenth and fifteenth to stand at three under. He rated his three at the fifteenth as his "birdie of the year," the result of a thrilling one iron, slightly faded into the squall and settling twelve feet behind the flag, from where he sank the putt. The excellence of that stroke was underlined when, at the short sixteenth, Langer's four iron straight into the wind carried no more than 140 yards, not even reaching the cross bunkers. He took four there and then five at the last, which was playing like a par five anyway.

And so a target of 141 was set, but a queue soon began to form. Senior, the Australian, was on the same mark after a 71 and here was another fine round considering he took seven at the seventeenth. His drive found the left hand bunker and he lost his recovery in the long grass. So he had to go back to the bunker and start all over again.

A 73 by young Lee, also for 141, revealed that he was by no means afraid of the big occasion and, indeed, he seemed to revel in it. Four bogeys in the space of eight holes beginning at the eighth might have rattled him, but they did not. He even began to think in terms of leading, and that did not frighten him either. He coped better with the weather than some.

Michael King, for instance, hoisted himself onto the leader boards when, after an opening round of 71, he moved to one under par for the championship with birdies at the twelfth and thirteenth. However, total collapse was soon at hand. At the fifteenth he drove into a bunker and got into such a mess that in the end the hole cost him a seven. At once he took five at the short sixteenth and then he ran into yet another double bogey at the last, which meant seven shots dropped in those last four holes and a 75 instead of the 68 it had briefly threatened to be.

Clark was another to fall foul of the fifteenth, taking six. He had until then been two under par, due largely to the eagle three he had at the seventh. The strength of the wind at his back was such that though he had 233 yards to the flag, he hit no more than a seven iron. Be judged it so well that he faced a putt of no more than a yard.

Another of the shots Clark dropped to par came at the fourth which even he, a long hitter, found utterly out of reach in two shots. But, as he neared the sanctuary of the clubhouse, Clark noticed not only a slight drop in the wind but also a rise in the temperature. It came just as the later starters were setting out and by degrees it began to throw a new slant on the championship. In a big field of more than 150 with starting times ranging between 7.30 a.m. and 4.30 p.m., the climate can change so swiftly that it might almost be a different country.

By then it had already become clear that this was not to be Ballesteros' year again. Though he had once again started with a birdie and then gone two under for the round with a four at the seventh, where like Clark he found a seven iron for his second sufficient club, he was unable to build on the beginnings of a recovery.

One of the difficulties at Royal St George's is keeping the ball low through the wind, for there are so many humps to be negotiated that the ball must be given air just to clear them. It was one at the eighth which precipitated the Spaniard's further slide. A three iron after a drive to the right side of the fairway caught the sandhill twenty yards ahead of him and came to an abrupt halt, and that was an inevitable five. Even so, Ballesteros was out in 34, but he could make nothing of the inward half, even though he found all the fairways from the tee.

Ballesteros blamed it as much as anything on his putting. In the five strokes he dropped in an inward half of 40 he took three putts twice and missed another of a yard for a birdie at the fourteenth. But in many ways he seemed just to run out of steam, worn out by the continual blast of wind and rain and finishing five, four, five, five—which represented a stroke dropped in each case.

But for some the gods were more kindly disposed, though Lyle could be excused doubting it when, for the second time, he fell foul of the first hole. He missed the fairway off the tee and, though only in the semi-rough, found one of the front bunkers with his second. As luck would have it, he was also plugged under the face and he could not get out first time. A six was the most disheartening of starts.

Nor was Lyle's morale improved when at the third he missed the green slightly to the left, pitched up and then missed a putt of ten feet or so. At four over par for the championship, Lyle was in grave danger of losing contact, but the hole that turned it all around for him was the fourth, a wickedly difficult par four that even the strongest were struggling to reach in two.

Lyle got as close as anyone but struck his ap-

proach putt across the great swinging slope so short of the hole that he left himself with a second putt of a good seven yards. When it disappeared, dead centre, a great sense of relief engulfed him and suddenly Lyle was a new man.

In no time at all Lyle had struck a five iron to eight feet for a two at the Maiden, the sixth, eased a three wood and six iron to the seventh green for another birdie and then a seven iron to ten feet on the swirling ninth green for another three. His 35, level par, to the turn was a great filip.

By now the wind was easing noticeably and patches of blue sky were appearing where once it had only been grey and forbidding. Lyle's morale soared. Par followed par, and by the time he reached the fourteenth, the par five which had struck fear into the hearts of those preceding him, he thought he had a good chance of reaching the green in two. But, in going for the extra length with his drive, he tugged it left into the thick rough. He was still able to get over Suez in two, but a "flier" with a nine iron went through the green, and he missed quite a short putt to save par.

This was the only stroke Lyle dropped to par on the inward half, for such now was the almost dead calm that Lyle was able to play both the fifteenth and seventeenth with nine iron second shots. Furthermore he almost finished with a birdie, lipping out from ten feet.

Graham likewise had a 71 for 139, the same as Lyle, and the turning point of it was, he thought, the fourteenth. He was at that point one over par for the round and the five he made, when it could have been anything, kept his spirits up.

The Australian also hooked his drive and found a miserable lie in the hay. So much grass festooned itself around his club as he tried to hack clear that the ball squirted thirty yards in the wrong direction, and Graham still had to lay up short of Suez in three. But from there he drilled a one iron to the flat, featureless green before sinking the putt from ten yards. Par saved.

If this delighted Graham, so did his play of the eighth, when the wind was still fierce. He could not have hit his drive and two iron better and though the putt for a birdie eluded the hole, it kept him at one under for the round after a birdie at the second.

Two shots were then dropped in a row at the ninth and tenth, first because of three putts and then an errant eight iron to the green against the skyline. However, there was still a two to come at the sixteenth, and Graham would have led on his own but for the eight iron he left short at the seventeenth. From the bottom of the slope, he took three to get down with his putter. Still, it was a solid round by the Australian and, at thirty-nine, he was beginning to get the taste for a third major championship to add to his U.S. PGA of 1979 and U.S. Open of 1981.

Poor O'Connor had a nightmare time after his dream round the day before. Driving indifferently and enjoying no luck with his putter, he had six bogeys in nine holes, relieved only by a birdie at the fifth, 422 yards, which he played with a six iron from the tee and an eight iron to the green. More bogeys followed at the thirteenth and fourteenth, but a disintegrating round was relieved by a comforting birdie at the sixteenth, and O'Connor played the last four holes in one under par, which was something not many had done.

Johnstone came back well for his 72. He had dropped three strokes in a row from the fourth, but a birdie at the seventh and another at the thirteenth revived him, and at this stage he was playing really well. He had a chance to catch Lyle and Graham at the head of the field, but his two iron to the last caught the slope in front of the green and from there he took three putts.

Weibring, the big, gentle mannered American, impressed once more with a 71, and for a time young Wayne Riley, a young Australian who was in the last group of the day, had a chance to catch the leaders. But he could not quite maintain his surge over the closing holes. For all that a 70 was a fine round of golf, as was that by the lightweight Spaniard, Rodriguez.

The low round of the day had nevertheless come from Eamonn Darcy with a 68. He was out in 32 and home in 36. All day only three players had beaten par, Langer and Paul Oglesby, of America, being the others. Moreover only two had matched it. Royal St George's had certainly shown its teeth.

David Graham (top) and Sandy Lyle were joint leaders at 139

Sharing third at 140 were Tony Johnstone (top), Christy O'Connor Jr. (bottom left) and D. A. Weibring (bottom right)

Bernhard Langer fought the elements and was sixth with six others

His wife as his caddie, Peter Senior made a good start

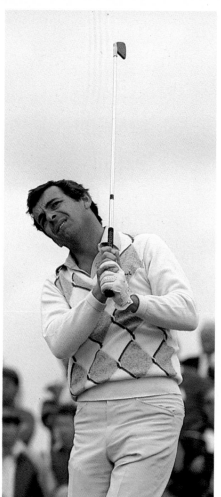

Jack Nicklaus (bottom) did not qualify after thirty-six holes, nor did other former champions Bill Rogers and Tony Jacklin (top left and centre) and Amateur champion Garth McGimpsey (right)

Eamonn Darcy's 68 enhanced Ireland's hopes

Payne Stewart trailed by six strokes

Paul Way (left) and Lanny Wadkins

Fuzzy Zoeller returned 76

COMMENTARY

Sandy Lyle: A Retrospective View

By David Davies

Sandy Lyle, amidst all the frenzied and frantic hopes his well-wishers had for him, remained as cool, as Raymond Chandler once said, as boarding house soup. His score was in. Only Bernhard Langer and David Graham could beat his 282 total and both needed a birdie, over Royal St George's fiendish finish, to prevent him becoming the first British winner of the Open Championship since Tony Jacklin sixteen years ago.

The wait lasted for thirty minutes. There was pandemonium in the press tent; chaos in the clubhouse; but around the man who mattered, Alexander Walter Barr Lyle, there was peace, perfect peace. Lyle, who makes phlegmatism seem like joy unconfined, calmly watched the television, phoned and talked about the situation with an almost unbearably excited father, and one by one saw all his rivals fail.

In the afternoon of Sunday 21 July, Lyle fulfilled a destiny and refuted an adage. Nice guys do win, and one just had.

At the age of three, some twenty-four years ago, Sandy Lyle struck his first golf ball—and sent it soaring eighty yards. "Hello" thought his father, "what have we here?"

What he had was an outrageously talented son; a son about whom Tony Jacklin said after the Open Championship had been won, "I have said it many times that I've never seen anyone who strikes the ball better, and I have played against every great player in the world who is living today."

The young Lyle was not rushed; neither was he pressured. He lived on the golf course at Hawkstone Park, a lovely place for a boy to grow up, with woods and ponds and climbable rocky outcrops. He was allowed his childhood by the people around him, the "A" team as they occasionally call themselves: father Alex, mother Agnes, sisters Alison and Anne.

He showed a continuing talent for the game and his interest was gently fostered and fueled by Alex Lyle, the professional these last thirty years at the club. Sandy was a big lad early on and so he formed a man's swing as a boy. It needed only a few adjustments as he grew into his early teens and his father, wisely, opted for only the occasional change. In those early days Lyle, aged thirteen and taking size eleven shoes, swung the club ultra-slowly, something he can still do. But his father wanted, eventually, a quicker tempo, a smoother rhythm that would be easier to maintain in all weather. He took his son through that radical change in easy stages, taking four or five winters to complete it, watching him win all along the way.

Eleven years ago I sat in the Lyles' living room talking to Sandy. "What," I asked him, "will you want to have achieved in ten years time?" His reply was almost casual. "Oh," he said, "I think I'd like to have won the Open Championship."

Perhaps no player in the history of British golf has dominated at so many levels. First at the regional level Lyle won the 1972 Midland Boys Championship, aged fourteen, and then became an England Boy International. In 1974 he won the Midland

Amateur Championship and the English County Champion of Champions event and in 1975, aged seventeen, he won representative honours for England at Boys, Youths and Senior levels.

That was the year he played in the Amateur Championship at Hoylake and met in the second round an aldermanic American, and beat him at the twentieth hole. As we walked back to the clubhouse, trying to console the victim of this precocious talent, I said "One day, you know, you may be proud to have been beaten by this boy." It was a pretentious thing to say, regretted the moment it came out, and not well received either. But I wonder, now . . .?

Lyle had become the amateur to beat in the whole country and no-one did it at Hollinwell where he took the English Open Amateur Stroke Play title, the Brabazon Trophy, beating, among others, the emergent Nick Faldo.

It was Lyle's first "classic" victory, achieved in the cheerful style that was to become a trademark. Over the last few holes, the championship developed into a match-play situation between Sandy and Geoff Marks, the Walker Cup golfer who was, at that time, as good a player as there was in Britain. Lyle had been two strokes ahead with three to play, but at the long seventeenth, Marks hit two enormous shots onto the green, some forty-five feet away. To great acclaim he holed the eagle putt.

I looked quickly across at Lyle, sitting on his haunches, surveying his own thirty footer, expecting to see a stricken young golfer.

Instead, Lyle was looking at Marks and *grinning* all over his face. He had enjoyed the moment and the absurdity of it, and was prepared to let it show. Then, as unconcerned as he still is in similar circumstances, he two-putted for a birdie and won the title by two shots when Marks took five at the last.

There was an inevitability about his progression made the more impressive by Lyle's total acceptance of it. Even then he treated triumph and disaster, the twin imposters as Kipling called them, in exactly the same fashion—neither seemed to matter that much. Hence right from those early days there have been the doubts, and the doubters, about Lyle's ability to take his talents to the heights. The conventional wisdom is that without the killer instinct you get nowhere; that you must be aggressive, pugnacious even to succeed.

There is nothing of that in Lyle. He remains the soft Shropshire lad that he was born; albeit with an inner steely Scottish resolve that comes from his Glaswegian parents. He seems able, however, to accept a round such as he had in the Irish Open just four weeks before he won at Sandwich when he

picked up his ball rather than take 90. And in the Swiss Open of 1983, he lost an eleven-shot lead with twenty-three holes to play and then lost the play-off to Nick Faldo when he missed a fourteen-inch putt at the second extra hole. Twenty minutes later, Lyle was sipping champagne, chatting to all and sundry, the calamity dismissed. There was ample room, then, for doubts.

But we are getting ahead of ourselves.

At seventeen, Lyle had the talent and the build to turn professional. But there was a sense of destiny abroad at Hawkstone Park. Alex Lyle was beginning to understand the depth of his son's abilities, was beginning to think already in historical terms and wanted Sandy to make all the stops along the way. That meant he must become a Walker Cup player and so he stayed with the amateurs until 1977, playing on the losing team at Shinnecock Hills. He turned professional, to the great relief of the other amateurs, in September of that year, and promptly won his first two assignments.

They were the PGA Tour Qualifying School and, in early 1978, the Nigerian Open. He had opening rounds of 61, 63 in that tournament, with its browns for greens and, if nothing else, had announced himself in spectacular fashion. He went on to become Rookie of the Year, although only forty-ninth in the money list and the wider golfing world wondered what they could expect of this lad and his prodigious hitting in 1979. The answer was, in many ways, his best year as a professional until 1985.

He won three tournaments, two in incredible fashion against the best golfers in Europe. His initial success came in the Jersey Open, with a limited field, but that gave him the confidence to go to Sweden for the Scandanavian Open. There, after two rounds, he found himself tied with Severiano Ballesteros and they played the last two rounds together. Ballesteros was to go on and win the Open Championship at Royal Lytham two weeks later, but he could not get past Lyle this week. Sandy covered the last nine holes of the third round in 30, to take a three-shot lead into the last round where, as expected, the Spaniard began to surge. He closed the gap to two and then, at the ninth, hit a little pitch and run to two feet for a certain birdie. Lyle, again unconcerned, pitched to six inches. He also birdied the tenth, then the eleventh, and won by a comfortable three shots.

Next the European Open. Lyle, one behind with one round to play, literally destroyed the field with six birdies in the first seven holes. It was the kind of run in which a player is almost helpless, as nice thing after nice thing happens to him, and it left

Lyle seven ahead of the field. He now needed a mental target to help protect that lead and he thought of Tom Watson's 65 when he beat Jack Nicklaus in the closing round of the 1977 Turnberry Open. "I'll go for that" he told himself and, standing on the eighteenth tee, needed a three to achieve it. He took a two iron deliberately, because Watson had; likewise a six iron for his second and he then holed his putt for an immensely impressive win.

That year he improved forty-eight places in the money list, to first, and he retained his European number one position in 1980. Lyle was to win tournaments in each of the next three years, but not with the regularity his talent should have delivered. He was, however, gathering himself. He married Christine Trew, a golf and swimming champion in her own right. They started a family, with Stuart; they moved down to Wentworth to be closer to Heathrow, and Dave Musgrove, the man who had carried Ballesteros' bag at Lytham in 1979, was recruited to the team.

Lyle's life was coming together nicely and the next explosion was scheduled for late 1984. He played seventy-two holes very competently in the Lancome Trophy at St Nom La Bretesche and came into the press tent to see by how many Ballesteros would win. He had a couple of glasses of red wine with Christine, who then totally stunned me by revealing that Sandy had played the entire tournament with a new grip, having changed from the Vardon to the interlocking style. No sooner was that said than Seve started dropping shots, four in the last six holes, and suddenly Lyle was in a play-off. No problem. A three wood, a wedge to fifteen feet, a putt and Sandy had won.

Most people winning like that would have considered it a gift, but Lyle drew confidence from having beaten the best player in the world. The grip change, a remarkable thing to do so late in his career, had worked—but then Sandy is so gifted you feel he could play with any grip. Just watch him sometime on the practice ground hitting eight-iron shots 150 yards left handed with the club reversed, to see what I mean. And he had, of course, reverted to Vardon by the time he got to Sandwich.

Off he went to Hawaii, to Maui for the Kapalua International, a tournament with a strong field and big money. He led after three rounds by three, went round in 65 in the final round and he won by eight shots from the likes of Craig Stadler, Bernhard Langer, Greg Norman, Lee Trevino, Andy Bean and Nick Faldo. He won £100,000.

From there to Japan where he came third in the Dunlop Phoenix and then rose again, so to speak, to win the Casio World Open again in a play-off, again with a birdie at the first, beating Gary Koch. He had won almost £200,000 in four tournaments but more importantly now knew within himself that he could beat the best, anywhere in the world, under the pressure of playing for big money.

The early days of 1985 were frustrating. Lyle threw himself into an American schedule that involved playing fourteen out of fifteen weeks and whilst in some events, like the Greater Greensboro Open, he was extremely impressive, he never quite had the breaks. It was the same when he came back to Europe, losing a play-off to Paul Way in the Whyte and Mackay PGA Championship and being nineteen under par in the French Open, only for Ballesteros to be twenty-one under.

Despite all that Lyle was in a good frame of mind when he arrived at Royal St George's. The course is one of his long-time favourites because of the necessity for long driving and good long iron play —both departments in which Lyle feels he excels. "If I'm going to win an Open," he told me before the start, "it'll be here or at Turnberry."

In that positive frame of mind Lyle played his first three rounds well and at the start of the fourth was three behind the leaders, just as Ballesteros, the previous year, had been two behind with eighteen to go.

There were, of course, 70 vital shots in that final round, but those played in the closing stages were the dramatic ones, the ones that will live in the memory.

Lyle's nerve, frequently questioned, served him well when he needed it most. That shot to the eighteenth was truly hit and was a little unlucky to trickle off the green. Then the little chip, which failed to get out of the hollow he was in...that too was a brave shot as Lyle tried for a delicate stroke to get the ball close the first time. "I played the shot well," he said afterwards. "I could have chickened out and banged the ball into the slope and gone thirty feet past the hole, but I wanted to try the proper shot."

In all the years I have known him Lyle has never evaded an issue on the golf course, much less lied about a shot and I totally accept his version of events.

They do him credit, just as he, by keeping his head and his hands steady has brought the best possible credit to all those close to him and to European golf in general.

THIRD ROUND RESULTS

Hole	1	2	3	4	5	6	7	8	9	10	11	12	13	14	15	16	17	18	Total	
Par	4	4	3	4	4	3	5	4	4	4	3	4	4	5	4	3	4	4	Total	
Bernhard Langer	4	3	3	4	5	2	5	4	3	4	3	4	4	5	4	2	4	5	−68	−209
David Graham	3	4	3	3	4	3	4	5	4	4	3	3	5	5	4	4	5	4	−70	−209
Mark O'Meara	4	3	4	4	4	3	4	4	4	4	3	4	4	5	4	3	4	5	−70	−212
Ian Woosnam	4	4	3	4	4	3	4	5	3	4	3	4	4	6	5	4	3	4	−71	−212
Christy O'Connor Jr	4	5	3	4	3	3	4	5	4	4	3	4	5	5	3	4	4	5	−72	−212
Sandy Lyle	4	4	2	4	4	4	4	5	4	5	4	4	4	5	4	3	5	4	−73	−212
Tom Kite	4	3	3	4	3	4	4	3	4	4	3	4	4	5	4	3	4	4	−67	−213
Peter Jacobsen	4	3	3	4	3	3	4	4	5	4	3	4	4	5	3	2	4	5	−68	−213
Greg Norman	4	4	2	4	4	3	4	5	4	4	3	4	5	5	5	3	3	5	−71	−214
D.A. Weibring	4	4	4	4	4	3	4	5	5	4	3	4	3	5	4	3	5	6	−74	−214

HOLE SUMMARY

Hole	Par	Eagles	Birdies	Pars	Bogeys	Higher	Rank	Average
1	4	0	6	60	17	3	8	4.20
2	4	0	14	51	20	1	14	4.12
3	3	0	7	61	18	0	10	3.13
4	4	0	9	58	18	1	13	4.13
5	4	0	12	58	16	0	17	4.05
6	3	0	7	65	13	1	14	3.09
7	5	1	42	39	3	1	18	4.55
8	4	0	7	41	33	5	3	4.42
9	4	0	10	53	19	4	6	4.21
Out	35	1	114	486	157	16		35.90
10	4	0	5	62	18	1	11	4.17
11	3	0	2	57	27	0	4	3.29
12	4	0	13	56	16	1	16	4.06
13	4	0	7	56	21	2	6	4.21
14	5	0	10	54	17	5	9	5.23
15	4	0	7	52	25	2	5	4.26
16	3	0	10	57	18	1	12	3.12
17	4	0	6	40	34	6	2	4.47
18	4	0	4	35	39	8	1	4.59
In	35	0	64	469	215	26		37.40
Total	70	1	178	955	372	42		73.30

LOW SCORES

Low First Nine	Bob Charles	32
	Mark James	32
	Tom Kite	32
	Sam Torrance	32
Low Second Nine	Ben Crenshaw	34
	Peter Fowler	34
	Peter Jacobsen	34
	Mark James	34
	Graham Marsh	34
	Chris Moody	34
	Jose-Maria Olazabal	34
	Jose Rivero	34
	Ove Sellberg	34
	Vaughan Somers	34
	Fuzzy Zoeller	34

Players Below Par	10
Players At Par	11
Players Above Par	65

Low Round	Mark James	66

THE THIRD DAY
Graham, Langer Set The Standard

By Michael Williams

Among the earliest risers at the Open Championship were Gordon Jeffrey, Chairman of the Championship Committee, and Alan Turner, who was responsible each day for setting the flag positions. Mr. Jeffrey has overall control and at 6 a.m., as a heavenly early morning sun rose across the Straits of Dover and into a clear blue sky, the daily telephone call was put in to the local meteorological office. Upon that depended, in some cases, where the flags were to be put and also the tee markers.

The report that reached the Royal and Ancient headquarters read: "The day will start dry with bright and sunny periods but this will soon change to cloud and heavy showers. The wind will become strong and blustery with a chance of thunder." There was further reference to the expected temperatures but it was the last sentence of the report that brought a frown on not a few foreheads. "The tail end of Hurricane Anna is expected to reach this area tomorrow afternoon."

Hurricane Anna, of no doubt American origin since hurricanes are much more common in the States than in Britain, had been wandering across the Atlantic for several days and was said to be somewhere south of Ireland. However her course was unpredictable, as was the speed of her progress. Mr. Jeffrey decided to play it safe and issued the following notice to competitors: "Due to the weather forecast and strengthening winds during the day, the Championship Committee has decided that the forward tee at the fourth hole will be used."

This was on the same line as the specially built championship tee but some thirty yards nearer the green, which reduced the hole to 440 yards. This contingency measure had been laid down earlier in the week, as had a forward tee at the seventh in 1981, though it never even entered conversation this week.

After two days of not the kindest weather the last thing the championship needed was a hurricane, but as the two leaders, Sandy Lyle and David Graham completed their session on the practice ground prior to driving off at 3.15 p.m., so the gathering storm clouds filled the sky. They had time to complete only the first hole, Graham with a birdie three and Lyle with a par four, before lightning, thunder and rain suspended play for an hour.

Happily, it did not turn out to be the early arrival of Hurricane Anna, and no-one was blown irretrievably off course. David Graham stood his ground at the head of the field with a 70, but the most significant move of the day had again seemed to come from Bernhard Langer, the new joint leader on 209.

Langer's 68 meant that he had scored progressively lower in each round (72, 69, 68) and to all intents and purposes the destiny of the championship lay between these two men. The bookmakers had decided as such even before they went out. Langer was five-to-two against and Graham five-to-one.

Lyle, though he had shared the lead after 36 holes, was ten-to-one and he now drifted back into a share of third place in the field as well on 212 with a 73, being caught by the American, Mark O'Meara (70), the Welshman, Ian Woosnam (71) and the Irishman, Christy O'Connor Jr (72).

O'Meara's was not the only warning shot by an

American. Tom Kite, who has always found a major championship so elusive, had a 67 and drew level with Peter Jacobsen (68), both now on 213 and four strokes behind the two leaders. Next, a stroke further away, were another American in D.A.Weibring (74) and an Australian in Greg Norman (71).

Mark Jamĕs, who has often reserved some of his best performances for the Open, improved by twelve strokes on his second round with a 66, and Lee Trevino conjured a 68. Out, in the second qualifying cut of the championship, went Gary Player, a triple champion from the past, Craig Stadler, Lanny Wadkins and the current leading European money winner, Paul Way.

Langer was on the fifth tee when the storm broke and sheltered at first in a hut. However, a German friend, staying in a house behind the fourth green, came over and invited him in for a cup of tea. Contrary to the assumption in some quarters, it is quite in order to leave the course in mid round, provided the player keeps his place in the field, which of course he will when play is suspended.

On the re-start Langer felt a little chilled and promptly dropped a stroke at the fifth, taking three putts from off the edge of the green. This cancelled out an earlier birdie at the second, but the West German was not long in the doldrums. He holed from six yards for a two at the sixth, saved his par brilliantly with a difficult chip from a downhill lie on the bank to the right of the eighth and then sank another long putt for a birdie at the ninth.

Out in 33, Langer was now in full cry. Two possible birdies got away at the tenth and twelfth, another chip saved him at the fifteenth and then he made not his first longish putt at the sixteenth for a two. However he could not get home with a three wood at the eighteenth, dragged the ball left and took five.

Having played in the penultimate match at St Andrews in the last round twelve months earlier, Langer was now assured of further elevation. It was something he relished, having had plenty of experience of it in Europe. Victory in the Masters earlier in the year had also taught him how to cope with the pressure. Everything about Langer suggested that he was ready for a championship that meant more to him than any other.

Graham had a good chance to have the lead on his own but took three putts at both the sixteenth and seventeenth, though the latter was admittedly from below the bank short of the green—much the same place as he had been the day before. Even so, he did not think that too much damage had been done.

Nevertheless these may have been tell-tale signs and Graham admitted to feeling a little "jumpy."

While not wishing to make excuses he did point out that "when you wake up at 10 o'clock and don't play until 3.15 and then finish between 7.30 and 8.0, your stomach tells you that it is time to eat and I had nothing to eat out there."

Certainly Graham's outward half was the better of the two. His three at the first, before the storm, was a cheering beginning and on the resumption he continued to play immaculately. An example of how much easier the fourth hole played from its forward tee was illustrated by the fact that Graham needed only a six iron for his second and he put it only two feet away for a second birdie. A third followed at the seventh, where he was on in two, and the only blemish came at the eighth. There he three-putted for a five, failing to guage the pace of the ridge between himself and the hole. Then came another birdie at the twelfth before the last five holes began to find a chink in his armour.

Graham was bunkered at the thirteenth, missed a very short—and for him irritating—second putt at the sixteenth and then, as already mentioned, took another three putts from short of the seventeenth. Again that second putt was on the short side and, by his action with his putter, the Australian seemed to be trying to tell the gallery that his ball had broke the wrong way. In the evening sunlight the pace of the greens had, he thought, changed and he could not make the adjustment.

All week Lyle had had difficulty in what he described as "getting the putter to work" and that was perhaps the main reason why he did not do better than 73. Even so that was only three strokes behind the leaders and, as Lyle said later, that sort of margin was really nothing on a course like this.

A beautifully shaped three iron to within a yard of the hole for a two at the third was a reassuring start to Lyle's round, but he was plugged in a bunker at the Maiden and took three putts at the eighth after the customary birdie at the long seventh.

Lyle's 35 strokes meant that he was two strokes behind Graham (33) and only level with Langer, also out in 33. Further decline followed, as Lyle thinned a recovery from wide of the tenth green down the slope the other side. He had to chip and single putt to avoid a six. Immediately he went through the eleventh green, chipped back well but missed the putt to take four.

There was a fine chance of a birdie at the thirteenth, but again Lyle missed, this time from not much more than a yard and, though he navigated the next four holes safely enough, he was twice in the "thick stuff" coming down the seventeenth and had to work hard for his five.

O'Connor, after his rather alarming 76 in the

second round, settled down again and played much better for his 72 for his share of third place. He did not feel at all nervous and while his round was not free of error, he kicked himself for only one of the shots he dropped.

Play was halted by the storm while he was on the second green, and at such moments a golfer has the option either of marking his ball or completing the hole. O'Connor chose to complete, but he also rushed the procedure, and it was this which accounted for him taking three putts.

There were other dropped shots at the eighth, thirteenth, sixteenth and eighteenth, missing the green at three of them and taking three putts again at the other (the sixteenth). Against that however came birdies at the fifth, seventh and fifteenth, the last of them being quite the best — a drive, five iron and putt of twenty feet.

O'Meara, who had won both the Bing Crosby Pro-Am and the Hawaiian Open on the U.S. tour this year, was making his second Open Championship appearance. The other was also at Sandwich in 1981. In the intervening years he had not played because he was required to pre-qualify and that was something he was not prepared to do. He made the suggestion that there ought to be a qualifying competition for the British Open in America and one in Britain for the U.S. Open. He believes it unreasonable to expect anyone to cross the Atlantic without any guarantee of competing in the championship.

Altogether it was an impressive round by O'Meara, and the American hit more greens than in either of the two previous rounds. Indeed the only ones he missed were the fourteenth, where he scrambled out with a par anyway after being short of Suez in two, and the eighteenth. The latter was not his only dropped shot, however, for earlier he had taken three putts at the third.

Woosnam's 71 was nothing like as neat. In fact all the credit lay with his touch on the greens. He had nine single putts and only twenty-eight in all. His only orthodox holes were the first, second, twelfth, thirteenth and eighteenth. A lot of those single putts were nevertheless quite short, which said a lot for his chipping. However, at the same time he was not missing the greens by much, and a golfer of his calibre would be reckoning to get down in two anyway.

There were four "saves" in a row from the fourth and two more at the tenth and eleventh. As well as those came single putts for birdies at the seventh and ninth but, in a somewhat ragged finish, Woosnam dropped three strokes in a row from the fourteenth before he holed yet another single putt

for a three at the seventeenth. Woosnam admitted that he has played better in his time but he was delighted to be so well placed and vowed to "go for everything" on the last day.

Kite's 67 was very possibly the finest round he had played all year. He is not known for his long hitting and therefore has to rely a lot on his short game. Yet on this big Royal St George's course, with the wind still blowing, he found no less than seventeen of the eighteen greens in the right number of strokes. He could not remember such a high ratio for a long time.

The one green Kite missed was the fifteenth, where he was short with a five iron, but he was close enough to be able to take his putter for his third shot, rolled it up to ten feet and sank the next. Even so Kite, who hardly seems to have aged at all since he played in the American Walker Cup team of 1971, could not escape the customary bogey somewhere. He took three putts for a four at the sixth. With four birdies, at the second, fifth, seventh and eighth he was nevertheless out in 32 and then came home in strict par. On his day he would have reckoned to have holed more putts than he did for he had a lot in the five- to six-yard range.

Jacobsen, who is among the most popular and likeable players on the U.S. tour, came back into the reckoning with his 68. While his nine at the fourteenth in the first round would take a lot of forgetting, he had made up his mind to be aggressive and attack the flag at all times.

It was a tactic that served Jacobsen well, and he was one under par when the storm clouds unleashed their fury just as he was playing the fifteenth. He just had time to hit a five iron to within a couple of feet of the hole and tap the putt in for his birdie. Two ice creams later, he struck a five iron to thirty feet and sank the putt, but the 67 for which he was on line eluded him as he drove into the rough at the last.

Not much had been heard of Norman, but the Australian had been consistent with rounds of 71, 72, 71 and was not afraid of the wind. So far he felt that he had played well without a lot of luck, and the five strokes by which he trailed Graham and Langer he regarded as by no means insurmountable.

James built his 66 on an outward half of 32 with four birdies in the first eight holes. It was a startling improvement on his 78 the day before, though most of that could be put down to the worst of the weather when it was so easy "just to take five." Perhaps the high spot of his round was a three at the last, where he chipped in. It was one of only four all day as the eighteenth maintained its rating as the hardest hole on the course.

Altogether ten players scored better than par and the first player to do so had been Lee Trevino, who would have been well in the hunt if he could have turned this into a seventeen-hole course by removing the eighth. In the second round the hole had cost him an eight and this time he took six. Even so he was round in 68.

Trevino was still smarting about that eight and did not forgive himself for taking 76 in what was, by his own admission, not the most difficult conditions. He had his feet up and was watching television when the other half of the field was pitting itself against the elements. Unlike probably any other player in the field, Trevino had not once taken three putts in three rounds, but he did concede that he has difficulty in maintaining his concentration these days. 'That eighth hole would never have happened fifteen years ago,' he said.

Fifteen years ago Arnold Palmer, Jack Nicklaus and Gary Player would have been expected to be in contention. But now Palmer was recovering from a minor operation in the States, and Nicklaus and Player were on their way home. Only Trevino, of the old guard, was still there.

U.S. Masters champion Bernhard Langer (next page) was joint leader after three rounds

David Graham (left) was a co-leader and Mark O'Meara shared third place, three strokes behind

Christy O'Connor Jr. (left) and Ian Woosnam were above par but in contention

Tom Kite (top left) and Sandy Lyle also had high hopes

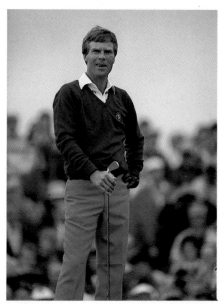

Peter Jacobsen (left) was well-placed at joint seventh, but countrymen Ben Crenshaw (centre) was nine strokes behind and Craig Stadler (right) did not qualify for the final round

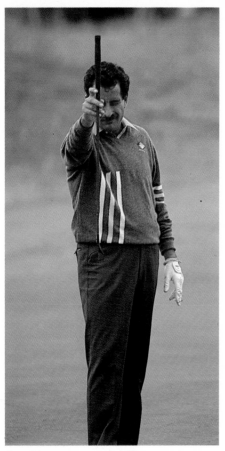

Sam Torrance returned 69   Mark James' 66 was low   Anders Forsbrand led the Swedes

Gary Player did not qualify for the final day

Lee Trevino had 68 in the third round

COMMENTARY
What The Open Is Meant To Be

By Michael McDonnell

The search for weighty significance to a championship in which the established stars falter and a flock of new candidates step forward can lead to some intriguing if arguable conclusions.

The easiest would be that we have come to the end of an era partly because most of the great players have edged past their prime and that golf itself at the very top is now full of many players of such similar standard that it is no longer possible to single out obvious winners.

This was not always true when considering the rare demands of a championship on a links where aspects other than mechanical skill are crucially important yet the scenario at Royal St George's demonstrated that those demands need no longer be met just by Americans and that the world in general —certainly Europe in particular—has caught up.

Lee Trevino made the point that while this was fact, it still stood as a tribute to the strength of American golf because the international players now emerging had all perfected their craft on the U.S. tour and that tradition had started back in the early days of Gary Player and continued on through Tony Jacklin, Severiano Ballesteros, Bernhard Langer and now Sandy Lyle.

Perhaps, too, another reason for golf's rapidly changing new order is that the demands at the very top are now too great and the rewards so huge that it is no longer possible nor necessary to sustain any kind of lengthy dominance or desire.

End-of-an-era theorists however point to the sad and premature departure of Jack Nicklaus, missing his first thirty-six-hole qualifying total in the Open in twenty-three years, growling about having the worst of the weather and in the nicest possible way making plain his views of Royal St George's by saying that his favourite courses were in Scotland and that in order of preference he then worked his way down through England and the Sandwich course is "the most southerly of them all!"

Of all the previous winners who slumped this time, Nicklaus was the most surprising although his form had dipped a month earlier when he missed the thirty-six-hole cut in the U.S. Open at Oakland Hills in Detroit. With due respect, nobody was much surprised when Tony Jacklin made an early exit in what was only his second competitive event of the year, nor for that matter when 1981 champion Bill Rogers, in the traumatic throes of questioning his role and future in the game, joined him.

By the end of the third round Gary Player, together with former U.S. Masters champion Craig Stadler and U.S. PGA champion Lanny Wadkins had also disappeared to support the "milestone" theory and there also signs that Severiano Ballesteros and Tom Watson had left things a little too late to catch up despite optimistic noises to the Press after each round.

Perhaps they too were smitten by a curious logic which attaches itself to any consideration of possible winners of a championship. It centres on the accepted need for what is called a "good winner" whose track record is beyond question, whose ability and class are proven and who, if he has not won before, was generally held to be pretty sure to do so soon.

Such a candidate then reaffirms the stature of the event and more importantly that of the championship course itself. Indeed when the Championship Committee met after the 1964 Open, won by Tony Lema at St Andrews, they considered the question of whether the Old Course had been out-dated by the improving skills and equipment of the modern golfer. They concluded that if the course sorted out and rewarded players of undisputed class then it still served its purpose and remained a relevant test with no serious weaknesses.

Since Jack Nicklaus took the 1978 Open there and Severiano Ballesteros captured the 1984 title, their case had been upheld.

The weakness however is that even champions of undisputed class had to be first-time winners at some time during their careers and such breakthrough victories—Ballesteros at Royal Lytham in 1979 for example—cannot be considered seriously as reflections on the course in question as though somebody has been allowed to slip through.

That said, several commentators suprisingly expressed personal difficulty in adjusting to the concept of Sandy Lyle acquiring the lofty status of Open champion as if his easy-going, day-to-day familiarity somehow disqualified him from being taken seriously even though few would argue that his playing skills, even before Royal St George's, ranked him among the world's best.

Yet the essence of the 1985 championship was that so many new champions could have emerged—men all of whom would have to be considered in a totally different light had they prevailed. There were ten of them covered by three strokes on that final afternoon though, in truth, not all of them were unaccustomed to the intense pressure of enduring the last crucial moments of a championship.

David Graham had the U.S. Open and the U.S. PGA titles to prove his worth and Bernhard Langer had stepped forward only months earlier from the pack to join the champions by taking the U.S. Masters at Augusta. Even Tom Kite who held the lead for a while on that last day fell into the "only-a-matter-of-time" category—a player of such formidable capability that a major title is inevitable.

All of them came close, actually holding the lead individually on the last afternoon, yet had the ball rolled perhaps fractionally differently, the world might have been obliged to adjust to an Open champion by the name of Payne Stewart, or Jose Rivero, or Christy O'Connor Jr, or Anders Forsbrand or D.A. Weibring.

All of them were involved in that final melee

when nobody knew from which direction the new champion would emerge. And that is the abiding strength of Royal St George's and why of all the championship courses it has made the Open joyfully "open" once again.

The victory by Bill Rogers back in 1981 made the point though its significance was missed. And it is not stretching the issue too much to suggest that Henry Cotton's 1934 triumph there after years of American domination was but part of the same phenomenon of Royal St George's.

Without question Sandy Lyle's triumph also demonstrated the genuine open-ness of the contest; no cosy elitism here with the acknowledged superstars playing amongst themselves as they did at St Andrews and Turnberry.

Royal St George's made them intensely vulnerable not simply in the way it examined their skills but for the rewards it offered to others who learned to answer its demands.

Thus the elite grumbled about old-fashioned aspects—blind shots, forbidding contours on fairways and greens, unfair tee shots that require the help of a radar screen to find the target! Yet the point must be made that not only does Royal St George's offer golf as originally intended but in the global scheme of things it possesses features that are essential to the test of a complete golfer.

Indeed, the reputation of a man who can win on the lushness of a U.S. Open course and then adapt to prevail on the imprecise and fast terrain of a links is beyond question—perhaps in the manner of a tennis player who triumphs on grass and clay.

Nor is it just a case of Royal St George's demanding what Henry Cotton called the ability to "hit to a stick" by which he meant knocking the ball to a marker-post and making compensations for wind strength and direction because there are no other clues to the route.

The task however even is more exacting than merely knowing the way, then hitting the shot. I stood behind the ninth green on that last afternoon and watched all the leaders pass by.

From the tee, it is not just a matter of hitting the fairway. The real target is a little, bowl-shaped hollow about 130 yards from the green and tucked in the left hand side of the fairway. It is the only place among the hills from which to have a fair chance of an even-stanced approach shot offering a possibility of the ball staying on the green.

But you have to know that hollow is there and you have to know precisely where to aim, wind direction and all, then be confident enough to hit the correct stroke to put the ball there. That is the unrelenting test of Royal St George's.

Perhaps more than any other championship course it observes the original values of testing the man as well as his golf. Any doubts that golf was never meant to be a fair game can be shed on its terrain. Many of its fairways have a spine running through them so they often reject a ball, even one that has been hit dead centre, and despatch it to the rough on either side.

Its weather, too, can be capricious and at times impossible. Yet while Ballesteros and Nicklaus could claim rightfully they got the worst of it for the first two days, Bernhard Langer found a way through the tempest with a 69 on the second day which must rank as one of the finest rounds played that week.

Such observations lead to an obvious conclusion that Lyle's triumph and the failure of the established players cannot be traced to any specific aspect—not the weather, nor the way he played the par threes or the par fives, nor even his strategy or that of others over the treacherous last four holes—the toughest part of the course—culminating in the most difficult hole of them all—the eighteenth itself. Truly, Royal St George's is not finished with you until your last putt is safely below ground.

Take two players of the calibre of Langer and Graham and ask them to get one birdie between them on the last four holes to secure a play-off. What happens? Graham, the more experienced, drops strokes at three holes. Langer drops shots at two of them and neither manages to finish even in second place.

The reason? Pressure, of course. The importance of the moment. But there is more to it than that. Those last four holes test almost every aspect of a player's repertoire just when he ought to be looking for a safe run down the finishing stretch. The course seems to make one last effort to spoil a score and most times achieves its objective.

Those closing holes certainly follow three points of the compass which means adjustments are necessary for a variety of wind positions. They demand full and precisely placed tee shots, and bravery to go for carries to exact positions on fiercely contoured greens. It is one of the most daunting finishes in golf — perhaps not as famed as the Old Course or Carnoustie — but equally savage and exhaustive.

Even Lyle himself was not immune as he faltered on the last to drop a stroke with that chip shot that rolled back off the green and brought him to his knees in frustration. That, too, prompted a peevish observation that a par-four on the last would have underlined his winning of the Open and not the losing of it by others.

What rot! Such views should first consider the double bogey with which Gary Player won the 1959 Open Championship at Muirfield. It was his first major. He went on to win nine of them. Walter Hagen, another winner at Royal St George's, got it right. It's not how. It's how many.

And perhaps what Royal St George's has restored to golf is a correct value and perspective on what the Open is meant to be. A great occasion of course but for all the pomp and circumstance, the basic purpose remains to determine which competitor can play best on the day.

Fine words and lofty significance may embellish that achievement for posterity, but the task is simply to find who can negotiate the test in fewest strokes. That week at Sandwich, it was Sandy Lyle.

Yet as he laid hands on the trophy, Sandy was obliged irrevocably to follow the other dictum of his predecessor Walter Hagen. You must win it again, to prove the first time was not just a fluke. Success, it seems, imposes its own harsh obligations. The comforting thought is that Sandy is equal to them.

FOURTH ROUND RESULTS

Hole	1	2	3	4	5	6	7	8	9	10	11	12	13	14	15	16	17	18	Total	
Par	4	4	3	4	4	3	5	4	4	4	3	4	4	5	4	3	4	4		
Sandy Lyle	5	4	3	4	4	3	4	4	4	4	3	4	5	4	3	3	4	5	−70	−282
Payne Stewart	3	4	3	4	4	3	4	4	5	4	3	4	3	5	4	3	4	4	−68	−283
Jose Rivero	4	3	2	4	3	3	4	4	4	4	4	4	4	5	4	4	4	4	−68	−284
Christy O'Connor Jr	4	4	3	4	5	3	4	4	4	4	3	4	4	5	5	4	4	4	−72	−284
Mark O'Meara	5	4	2	4	4	3	5	4	5	4	3	4	4	5	5	2	5	4	−72	−284
David Graham	5	4	3	5	5	3	4	4	4	3	4	4	4	5	5	4	4	5	−75	−284
Bernhard Langer	5	4	3	5	5	3	5	5	4	4	3	4	4	5	3	4	4	5	−75	−284
Anders Forsbrand	4	4	4	4	5	2	5	4	4	3	3	4	4	5	4	3	4	4	−70	−285
D.A. Weibring	4	5	3	4	4	3	4	4	4	4	3	3	4	5	4	4	4	5	−71	−285
Tom Kite	4	4	2	4	4	2	4	4	4	6	3	4	5	5	4	3	5	5	−72	−285

HOLE SUMMARY

Hole	Par	Eagles	Birdies	Pars	Bogeys	Higher	Rank	Average
1	4	0	4	37	20	0	7	4.26
2	4	0	9	47	5	0	16	3.93
3	3	0	8	41	11	1	14	3.08
4	4	0	4	31	21	5	2	4.44
5	4	0	5	39	17	0	10	4.20
6	3	0	8	41	12	0	15	3.07
7	5	2	28	30	1	0	18	4.49
8	4	0	1	36	21	3	2	4.44
9	4	0	5	40	13	3	8	4.25
Out	35	2	72	342	121	12		36.16
10	4	0	7	41	10	3	11	4.15
11	3	0	2	47	12	0	9	3.16
12	4	0	3	46	11	0	12	4.13
13	4	0	4	45	10	1	12	4.13
14	5	1	15	42	0	2	17	4.78
15	4	0	4	33	21	2	4	4.35
16	3	0	4	40	16	0	6	3.20
17	4	0	2	39	19	0	5	4.28
18	4	0	0	28	31	1	1	4.55
In	35	1	41	361	130	9		36.73
Total	70	3	113	703	251	21		72.89

LOW SCORES

Low First Nine	Jose Rivero	31
Low Second Nine	Eamonn Darcy	33
Low Round	Eamonn Darcy	68
	Philip Parkin	68
	Jose Rivero	68
	Payne Stewart	68

Players Below Par	7
Players At Par	6
Players Above Par	47

THE FOURTH DAY
A Young Boy's Dream Is Realised

By Michael Williams

The eyes of the eleven-year-old boy who sat in the grandstand beside the eighteenth green at Royal Lytham in 1969 shone with excitement. Before him Tony Jacklin struck a peerless drive far beyond the cross bunkers to the middle of the fairway, a seven iron to the green, and two putts later, Britain had its first Open champion for eighteen years.

As Jacklin removed his ball from the hole and tossed it exultantly to the cheering crowd, so it arched towards the stand where the boy now stood. For a moment he thought that he would catch it, but it fell short into other eager fingers and the boy left empty handed. In his young mind, however, there was now a dream for already he was a golfer, the son indeed of a professional.

Now, sixteen years on, that same boy had become a man and his dream had also come true as, with a broad grin on his face, he walked through an avenue of backslaps to the eighteenth green at Royal St George's to acknowledge the thunderous applause as the multitude acclaimed Sandy Lyle its Open champion.

No other British golfer since Jacklin had won the championship, but the circumstances of these twin landmarks were entirely different. Whereas Jacklin had led by two strokes going into the final round, his victory an intensifying climax as the crowd held its breath and crossed its fingers all that last afternoon, Lyle's opportunity did not beckon until the last five holes. And then it was he who held his breath.

When Lyle putted out on the eighteenth green, he was not necessarily the champion for Bernhard Langer, of West Germany, and David Graham, of Australia, were still out on the course and either of them could still catch him, or even beat him.

Lyle therefore had to endure an agonising half-hour wait, his destiny now beyond his own control. He watched the television in the score recorder's hut and even found time to ring his parents in their Shropshire home, though none of them knew what to say.

But at length it became clear that both Langer and Graham needed birdie threes to tie and when both of them took five at the eighteenth, they even fell back into a five-way tie for third place behind Payne Stewart, of America, who had made a late surge with a final round of 68.

So Lyle's final level-par round of 70 on a day when Hurricane Anna's forecast arrival failed to materialise was good enough to win him his first major championship at the age of twenty-seven. His prize was a record for the Open of £65,000, though the ultimate rewards will be far in excess of that. His total, 282 for the four rounds, was the first time the championship had been won with a score of over par since Gary Player's 289 at Carnoustie in 1968.

Such are mere details within the tapestry of an involved afternoon when it was seldom clear who was going to win. Graham and Langer shared the lead for a time, until the American, Tom Kite, wrested it from them. Then Graham regained it again before Lyle at last forged ahead and, unlike the others, held on. For one awful moment, right at the very end, he thought he had let slip an opportunity that might never come again.

As Lyle came down the eighteenth fairway, the stands packed around the green, he led by a stroke from both Langer and Graham, who were now about to play the sixteenth. The cards were therefore in his hand and he knew that a four at the last would almost certainly be enough to ensure his cherished triumph.

A fine drive down the right hand side of the fairway left him with no more than a six iron to the green, but the shot failed to move left to right as it was intended to do. Lyle's ball kicked down into what is known as Duncan's Hollow, an awkward little swale from which many have had a lot of difficulty over the years.

However Lyle's ball was lying reasonably and, in a breathless hush, he tried to judge the chip so that it just climbed the crest before rolling gently on to the flag. By a fraction Lyle miscalculated. His ball did not quite reach the top of the slope and, to a groan that must have echoed all over Britain, it slid slowly back again to the edge of the green.

No golfer is less demonstrative or more philosophical than Lyle, but the agony of it all was too much even for him. As his ball made its return journey towards him, Lyle sank to his knees and buried his head in the grass. He still got down in two more for his five, but in those fleeting seconds he thought the opportunity had gone and, at best, he might be in a play-off.

If this was a slight anti-climax, so, too, it must be said, were the rounds of both Langer and Graham. Tieing the lead as they were three strokes ahead of the field going into the last round, it was totally unpredictable that both should then take as many as 75. It was almost a case of their having eyes only for one another, and then waking up too late for the threat that was coming from other quarters.

There were early tell-tale signs. There had been those two short putts Graham had missed towards the end of his third round, and now he resumed by driving into the rough on the right of the first fairway. The lie was bad and the Australian's recovery merely careered across the fairway, leaving him with a longish pitch to the green. There was one stroke gone.

Langer, by now the four-to-five favourite (Graham was five-to-four, Mark O'Meara eight-to-one and Lyle ten-to-one), had meanwhile driven straight and true. His pitch was a fraction too strong, but it was not a difficult chip, and he laid it not much more than a yard from the hole. If once that length of putt had given Langer nightmares, he did not suffer them any longer. But he missed it

all the same, and the seed of doubt was there.

Safe pars followed but at the fourth Langer missed the green on the left with his second. He could not get down in two more, while Graham took three putts from the bottom of the slope. Suddenly the championship was no longer a two-horse race and, when both followed it with fives at the fifth, the door was wide open for others to step through.

Kite, who had that splendid 67 on Friday, was the first to take the opportunity. Still in the same vein of form, he had played immaculately with birdie twos at the third and sixth, neither on long putts after perfect mid-iron shots, and then another at the seventh, where he was on in two. There was a bit of a scramble for his par at the ninth but he was out in 32 and two strokes clear of the field.

The fair-haired, bespectacled American had now played twenty-seven successive holes in ninety-nine strokes but no sooner had the vision of his first major championship appeared than it disappeared in the space of one hole, the tenth. Kite missed the green left and faced a steep pitch up and over a bunker to the green high above him. Normally it would have been a straight-forward shot for Kite but no shot is ever straight-forward as the Open nears its climax. He fluffed it into the bunker, thinned the recovery through the green and in the end had to hole from a good six feet to avoid a seven.

His six was nevertheless a heavy body-blow, and for Kite the spell had been broken. He was through the thirteenth green in two and took three more to get down; he took three putts from the very front of the seventeenth green and could not salvage his par from the left of the eighteenth green. So that was a 72 for Kite and in the end he shared no better than eighth place with Anders Forsbrand, of Sweden, and D.A. Weibring, of America.

Kite's departure from the top of the leaderboard made room again for Graham, who had partially recovered from those three bogeys in the first five holes with a birdie at the seventh and then, less predictably, at the tenth, where a putt of some forty feet never looked other than in the hole from the moment it left the clubface.

Langer had no such relief, running up his fourth bogey of the round at the eighth, where he found a bunker with his second, and struggling on through more sand at the ninth and tenth, though this time without cost. His 39 to the turn was a heavy burden and at this point he had been overtaken by both Lyle and Christy O'Connor Jr, both of whom were out in 35 with a birdie and a bogey apiece but seemingly unable to make any inroads on par.

If anything O'Connor looked the more likely to

find a way of breaking through. His head would roll left and right as if to assist his shots to find their targets, but he was no more rewarded with his putting than Lyle had been all week. Still the pars kept coming, but no birdies and Lyle suffered what seemed at the time to be a mortal blow as he took five at the thirteenth. He drove into a bunker, had a chance of finding the green with his recovery but missed it and had to work hard for his bogey as he sent his chip scuttling through the green.

With Graham also dropping a shot at the eleventh, where he was bunkered on the right, there was suddenly the prospect of the championship falling into the lap of Stewart, an American with experience of the European tour and one noted for his preference for plus twos and a liking for pastel colours.

As Stewart had begun this final round six strokes behind the leaders, no-one had given him much of a thought but his 68, to follow earlier rounds of 70, 75 and 70, lifted him from a share of eleventh place to the top of the leaderboard. With those still out on the course making so few positive moves, there was a real possibility that Stewart's total of 283 might stand up to the end.

Stewart was nevertheless kicking himself for not having set an even more difficult target. Having played the first seven holes in two under par, he then hit a five iron to within two and a half feet of the flag on the eighth and looked certain to go three under for the round. Somehow the putt got away however and perhaps it played on his mind. At all events he did the same thing again at the ninth, this time when he was trying to save par after missing the green with a five iron.

Still, 34 to the turn had certainly put Stewart in the reckoning, and he soon got back into his rhythm again with some solid pars and then a birdie at the thirteenth, where he holed from fifteen feet. Stewart had surprised even himself, for he gradually felt more and more pressure and the weather had made it even harder. Mentally drained, it was just a relief that he could now sit back and watch others try to beat him.

If one battle was now over, the war was not, and it was at about this time that Lyle, who had seen the title disappearing from view at the thirteenth, brought it back into focus again at the fourteenth. The circumstances surrounding it could hardly have been less likely. At the fourteenth he hooked into such heavy rough that even a man of his strength and powers of recovery could not contemplate carrying the canal with his second. He played out short and now, still more than 200 yards from the green, was struggling to save par. Instead he unleashed a two iron and of all things holed the putt for a birdie four from twenty feet.

With those two strokes, Lyle was back in the running again and three more equally telling ones were to follow immediately. At the treacherous fifteenth, he hit a drive and six iron to twelve feet and, as he contemplated the putt, he knew with absolute certainty that it could be the most crucial of his life. When it went in he was, he admitted later, close to tears with joy.

To have stood, as Lyle had done, on the tee side of Suez and walked on to the sixteenth tee five strokes later was a quite astounding sequence of golf at such a moment. Now he was ahead on his own and if only he could now play the last three holes in par, he knew that the dream of that eleven-year-old boy in the grandstand at Royal Lytham sixteen years earlier had every chance of coming true.

Two testing second putts were safely sunk at the sixteenth and seventeenth for a three and four and only the three shots he took to get down from the edge of the eighteenth left him in an agony of suspense. The hushed crowd around the green glued its eyes to the scoreboard and awaited Langer and Graham, who alone could now catch or beat him.

The two were tied, Graham having driven into a bunker at the fifteenth, which made a five inevitable, whereas Langer, fine competitor that he is, drew level at the same hole with his solitary birdie of the afternoon. He was home with a one iron second and sank the putt from around five yards.

At once they slipped again. Langer found a bunker to the right of the green with his tee shot — and furthermore was plugged —while Graham was even wider to the right. Neither could save their threes and both therefore needed one birdie from the last two holes to tie. They got their fours at the seventeenth and that left them with a birdie at the last to tie.

Graham was bunkered in two beside the green, but Langer played a thrillingly bold shot with a four iron and just ran through to the fringe. The chip he faced was his last chance and he put everything he had into it, his ball brushing the hole as it ran past. He deserved a four but, like Graham, instead took five.

So both fell back into a tie for third place with the Spaniard, Jose Rivero (68), the American, O'Meara (72) and the gallant O'Connor (72). All were on 284, four over par.

But it was Lyle the crowds were now acclaiming.

FINAL LEADERS

Sandy Lyle	282
Payne Stewart	283
Jose Rivero	284
Christy O'Connor Jr	284
Mark O'Meara	284
David Graham	284
Bernhard Langer	284
Anders Forsbrand	285
D.A. Weibring	285
Tom Kite	285

ATTENDANCE

Sunday	464
Monday	1,121
Tuesday	7,332
Wednesday	10,553
Thursday	28,000
Friday	32,881
Saturday	29,609
Sunday	28,067
	138,027

CHAMPIONSHIP HOLE SUMMARY

Hole	Par	Eagles	Birdies	Pars	Bogeys	Higher	Rank	Average
1	4	0	25	270	147	11	6	4.32
2	4	1	74	314	60	4	17	3.99
3	3	0	41	275	130	7	7	3.23
4	4	0	26	200	171	56	2	4.60
5	4	0	50	319	81	3	16	4.08
6	3	0	47	302	96	8	12	3.15
7	5	15	209	206	22	1	18	4.53
8	4	0	21	213	178	41	3	4.55
9	4	0	50	274	107	22	11	4.23
Out	35	16	543	2373	992	153		36.68
10	4	0	45	263	122	23	8	4.28
11	3	0	35	297	113	8	8	3.21
12	4	0	48	302	91	11	14	4.14
13	4	0	33	292	114	13	10	4.24
14	5	1	70	269	80	32	13	5.19
15	4	0	30	239	155	28	5	4.41
16	3	0	53	306	87	6	15	3.10
17	4	0	18	250	163	21	4	4.42
18	4	0	13	177	231	31	1	4.62
In	35	1	345	2395	1156	173		37.61
Total	70	17	888	4768	2148	326		74.29

	First Round	Second Round	Third Round	Fourth Round	Total
Players Below Par	11	3	10	7	31
Players At Par	12	2	11	6	31
Players Above Par	130	148	65	47	390

THE CHAMPION'S CARD

Round	Hole	1	2	3	4	5	6	7	8	9	10	11	12	13	14	15	16	17	18	Total
	Par	4	4	3	4	4	3	5	4	4	4	3	4	4	5	4	3	4	4	−70
One		5	4	3	4	3	3	4	4	4	5	3	3	3	5	4	3	4	4	−68
Two		6	4	4	4	4	2	4	4	3	4	3	4	4	6	4	3	4	4	−71
Three		4	4	2	4	4	4	4	5	4	5	4	4	4	5	4	3	5	4	−73
Four		5	4	3	4	4	3	4	4	4	4	3	4	5	4	3	3	4	5	−70

Mark O'Meara (top left) shared third place with four others. Tom Kite (top and bottom right) led until taking double bogey on the tenth. Payne Stewart's (bottom left) 68 was enough for second place

Christy O'Connor Jr. placed joint third

Jose Rivero (top) was joint third and
Jose-Maria Olazabal was the low
amateur

Bernhard Langer (left) and David Graham made desperate efforts to tie Lyle on the last hole. They finished joint third

Sandy Lyle's crucial birdie at the fifteenth (above) and his missed birdie putt at the sixteenth (left)

Lyle struggled to make five from Duncan's Hollow at the eighteenth

Triumphant Sandy
Lyle with R & A
Secretary Michael
Bonallack (left)
and Gordon
Jeffrey, Chairman
of the Champion-
ship Committee

Christine and
young Stuart Lyle
made it a family
celebration

COMMENTARY
In Search Of A British Champion

By John Hopkins

In July 1969 I was in Paris for a week-end when I heard the news that Tony Jacklin was leading the Open Championship after three rounds. On the Sunday morning I hurried down to the Gare St Lazaire and at a newspaper stall asked in my best French for the English papers. Coincidentally, only one was available, *The Sunday Times.* I handed over my money and turned anxiously to the sports pages. My eyes skimmed the cricket, passed over the tennis and settled on this reassuring headline: "Gentlemen, the toast is Tony Jacklin!" Beneath, in a wodge of black type ran a sub-head, which read: "One of golf's most memorable moments since the war —when Britain hailed a home-grown champion!"

In the years that followed Britain did not hail another home-grown champion. Jacklin himself went close to a second victory and Peter Oosterhuis was only pipped at the post but, year after year, the winner was an American, a South African, a Spaniard, anyone, it seemed, but someone from Britain or Ireland. It was all very frustrating. The home islands longed for a champion we could call our own as the Australians wanted the America's Cup. Now at last it has happened. Australia holds the America's Cup and Britain has an Open champion. "Gentlemen, the toast is Sandy Lyle!"

For a day that was to end so momentously, it all began in rather commonplace fashion. The weather relented and gave us a still, slightly overcast morning which promised rather less foul weather than had been delivered on the three previous days.

In his rented cottage in Sandwich, Lyle amused his son Stuart by playing with the Lego Stuart had received for his second birthday two days earlier. Not far away, the house the Langers were renting resounded to the sounds created by Bernhard and his wife Vikki, her sister and brother-in-law who were in Britain on honeymoon, Langer's brother Erwin and his wife and another couple. Only Willi Hoffmann, Langer's coach, was missing from the entourage of the Masters champion. Hoffmann had had to return to his club job at Stuttgart golf club.

Over breakfast I made my plans for the day. I was going to follow Langer and David Graham, the last pair out, reasoning that one or other of them would become champion. In my heart I felt it would be Langer, who had come through the field with a rush after an opening 72 had left him thirty-ninth equal. He had an air about him that suggested he meant business, as much as to say that in the third of golf's annual major events he was determined to repeat his Augusta triumph. In addition, I was influenced by Hoffmann who said he thought that Langer was swinging marvelously after watching his protege in practice.

But if it wasn't to be Langer then I felt sure it would be Graham, whose rounds of 68, 71 and 70 placed him second equal and then first equal. Graham is a graduate of the hard bastard school, one who gives nothing away, not even a beer and certainly not his hard-won share of the lead in a golf tournament. Remembering how he had hit all but one of the fairways and all the greens in regulation in the last round of the 1981 U.S. Open at Merion, which he won, I thought to myself, "He's good enough for me."

I didn't fancy the chances of the first day's hero Christy O'Connor Jr nor Ian Woosnam though the little Welshman had adopted a sensible attitude to the last day's play. "I'll go for everything" he had said the previous night when he lay third. "If it comes off that'll be the Open Championship. If it doesn't then so be it." I noted the menacing presence of Mark O'Meara, Peter Jacobsen and Tom Kite and decided to keep an eye on them. Of the Americans, only D.A. Weibring had been in the leading twelve players at halfway. And Sandy Lyle? On the last day at Troon in 1982, Lyle had been one of a group close to the leaders and, over breakfast, David Graham had voiced his fear of the Scot. "He's so bloody long" growled Graham.

There were doubts in my mind about Lyle, however. He was driving long and straight, and was putting well, and when these two aspects come together then the sparks usually fly. But in the last round of an Open Championship, when some of the most experienced players in the world were bunched around him? To be quite honest, I not only doubted Lyle's chances, I scarcely gave them a second thought.

Langer and Graham put the finishing touches to their preparation, and then came together on the putting green to wish one another luck. Langer, strikingly smart in his white flannels and blue sweater, looked like a man who believed in himself. It took five holes before I finally accepted that neither of them was going to be a factor—at least not yet. In this time they had each missed three greens and squandered three shots. Kite was the leader according to the scoreboard at the back of the fifth green. It was time to make a move.

At moments like this, golf correspondents need to be fit. Waiting only to hear the roars that greeted first Graham's and then Langer's tee shots to the short sixth, and thinking that I might be leaving them at precisely the turning point of their fortunes, I took off in search of Kite. I darted across the seventh fairway when a steward was looking the other way, passed Ian Woosnam and Mark O'Meara on the eighth green, and then ran down into the hollow that sheltered the knot of catering tents and toilets. On I ran, out and up the other side until I reached the tenth green. Soon, spectators rushing from the ninth to the tenth fairway foretold the arrival of Kite, who was still tournament leader.

Journalists often seem to carry a hex with them, as well as a notepad and portable typewriter.

Thus, a colleague who went to visit Sebastian Coe on the eve of an attempt on a world record, sent him down with 'flu. No sooner had I caught my first glimpse of Kite than he went into perilous decline. He pulled his approach shot, underhit a chip, thinned a bunker shot. Need I go on? My hex was working, and by the time Kite left the green he had slumped to plus two, and Graham held the lead again.

I decided to make another cross-country run, this time to catch Lyle at the fifteenth and when I arrived at this green I confronted another delicate problem. The first had been which match to follow. Having resolved that, I now had to effect an entry to the greenside position I was entitled to take up. I slipped a shoulder between two spectators and said "excuse me" expecting them to part, like the Red Sea. They didn't move. I pulled back and passed on. I tried the same technique further around the line of spectators. This time it worked, though I had to prise my way past a reluctant couple in the front row. I threw myself down onto the grass, making sure that I kept the highest point of my body below the tops of the longest blades of grass. Nevertheless a voice rang out: "'Ere, out the road." I shuffled sideways until I no longer blocked anyone's view although I felt as if I was the front man on a bobsleigh descending the Cresta run instead of a golf correspondent.

Lyle and O'Connor came and went, Lyle holeing for a birdie and O'Connor seeming to relish every moment of it. "It was a great crack" he would say later. Then it was time to move on though not before another friendly sally floated my way. As we journalists and posse of photographers moved on to the sixteenth tee, a loud voice was heard to say: "There go the parasites."

It's history now what Lyle did over those closing holes. As the spectators saluted him from every quarter, and as his wife Christine embraced him after she made a hectic dash to the course piloted by Howard Clark, I stood by the side of the last green somewhat disappointed. I had hoped that the first Briton I had ever seen win the Open Championship would have done it in rather more style.

Circumstances beyond Lyle's control made St George's a less popular Open venue and this was a reason why so few Americans chose to attend the event. Why, you could almost hear them saying to one another, there isn't a flat fairway on the course. It's like the surface of the moon. It is worth speculating that the rise in European golf may have frightened off a few of the old war horses, those who traditionally used the Open as a place to earn the money with which they could take tea at Harrods and buy a year's supply of cashmeres.

There was nothing Lyle could do about being in the third from last group on this fateful day. But how I wish he could have won the victory he will undoubtedly cherish for the rest of his life by ripping an iron into the heart of the last green for a birdie or even by taking a cast-iron par four. As it was, most of the drama of the last hour's play was invested in the moments surrounding Lyle's poor chip at the last.

When his ball failed to reach that evil-looking crest in the green and rolled back to his feet, Lyle showed how angry he felt by uncharacteristically sinking to his knees and resting his head on the ground, a gesture worthy of Seve Ballesteros in its extravagance. At that moment I was crouching next to a stout lady seated on a shooting stick. She gasped as she saw the result of Lyle's chip and I'm afraid that I thought to myself "another gallant British effort." Then Lyle, never one to play to the gallery, struck a brilliant shot. The trouble is that he played it so quickly we hardly realised he had done it. He caressed his first putt up the slope so that it died within two feet of the flag. After O'Connor had sportingly quietened the crowd, Lyle holed out for what turned out to be an historic victory.

I am delighted that he won. It could not have happened to a nicer bloke nor one who is more down to earth. It is entirely appropriate for such a man that at breakfast that morning he had said that if he won, he would erect a marquee in his garden at home and invite his friends and the Press. More than most players, Lyle has many of the former among the latter. He is a man with whom it is so easy to identify that everyone who knew of his success at Sandwich, and a good many who didn't as well, could not but warm to him being interviewed by Terry Wogan while wearing a suit that was slightly too big and while his shirt collar rode up over a lapel of his jacket and his tie was rather skew whiff around his neck.

There's a man who won't be changed by success, I thought to myself as I watched him speaking sincerely and simply on television. I hope that Sandy Lyle becomes a millionaire and buys several more of those cross country motor bikes he likes to ride around on a patch of rough ground near his parents house in Shropshire. But it was a disappointment that this longed-for triumph came about the way it did, less heroically than Lyle deserved and less bravely than Jacklin's all those long years ago.

FINAL RESULTS

Hole	1	2	3	4	5	6	7	8	9	10	11	12	13	14	15	16	17	18	
Par	4	4	3	4	4	3	5	4	4	4	3	4	4	5	4	3	4	4	Total
SANDY LYLE																			
Round 1	5	4	3	4	3	3	4	4	4	5	3	3	3	5	4	3	4	4	68
Round 2	6	4	4	4	4	2	4	4	3	4	3	4	4	6	4	3	4	4	71
Round 3	4	4	2	4	4	4	5	4	5	4	4	4	5	4	3	5	4		73
Round 4	5	4	3	4	4	3	4	4	4	4	3	4	5	4	3	3	4	5	70	282
PAYNE STEWART																			
Round 1	4	4	4	4	4	3	4	4	4	4	3	4	4	4	4	3	5	4	70
Round 2	4	4	3	6	5	4	4	5	4	4	3	4	4	5	5	3	4	4	75
Round 3	4	4	3	4	4	3	4	4	4	4	4	4	4	6	4	3	3	4	70
Round 4	3	4	3	4	4	3	4	4	5	4	3	4	3	5	4	3	4	4	68	283
JOSE RIVERO																			
Round 1	5	4	3	5	4	4	4	5	4	3	4	4	4	4	5	3	4	5	74
Round 2	4	3	3	5	4	4	4	5	4	5	2	4	4	5	4	3	5	4	72
Round 3	3	4	3	5	4	3	5	5	4	4	3	4	3	5	4	3	4	4	70
Round 4	4	3	2	4	3	3	4	4	4	4	4	4	4	5	4	4	4	4	68	284
CHRISTY O'CONNOR JR																			
Round 1	5	3	4	3	3	2	4	3	3	3	3	3	5	5	5	3	3	4	64
Round 2	5	4	4	5	3	3	6	5	5	4	3	4	5	6	4	2	4	4	76
Round 3	4	5	3	4	3	3	4	5	4	4	3	4	5	5	3	4	4	5	72
Round 4	4	4	3	4	5	3	4	4	4	4	3	4	4	5	5	4	4	4	72	284
MARK O'MEARA																			
Round 1	5	4	3	3	4	3	5	4	4	5	2	4	3	7	4	2	4	4	70
Round 2	5	4	3	5	4	4	5	4	4	4	3	3	4	5	4	3	4	4	72
Round 3	4	3	4	4	4	3	4	4	4	4	3	4	4	5	4	3	4	5	70
Round 4	5	4	2	4	4	3	5	4	5	4	3	4	4	5	5	2	5	4	72	284
DAVID GRAHAM																			
Round 1	4	4	4	4	4	3	4	4	5	5	3	3	4	5	3	2	4	4	68
Round 2	4	3	3	4	4	3	5	4	5	5	3	4	4	5	4	2	5	4	71
Round 3	3	4	3	3	4	3	4	5	4	4	3	3	5	5	4	4	5	4	70
Round 4	5	4	3	5	5	3	4	4	4	3	4	4	4	5	5	4	4	5	75	284
BERNHARD LANGER																			
Round 1	5	4	2	4	3	4	4	4	4	4	3	4	5	4	7	3	4	4	72
Round 2	4	3	3	4	4	3	4	5	4	4	3	4	4	4	3	4	4	5	69
Round 3	4	3	3	4	5	2	5	4	3	4	3	4	4	5	4	2	4	5	68
Round 4	5	4	3	5	5	3	5	5	4	4	3	4	4	5	3	4	4	5	75	284
ANDERS FORSBRAND																			
Round 1	4	4	3	4	4	3	4	4	4	4	3	4	4	5	5	3	4	4	70
Round 2	4	4	4	5	4	3	4	5	4	5	3	4	4	5	4	3	6	5	76
Round 3	4	4	3	4	4	3	4	5	3	4	3	4	4	4	4	4	4	4	69
Round 4	4	4	4	4	5	2	5	4	4	3	3	4	4	5	4	3	4	4	70	285
D.A. WEIBRING																			
Round 1	4	4	4	4	4	2	6	4	3	4	3	4	4	5	5	3	3	3	69
Round 2	4	4	3	5	4	3	5	4	4	5	4	4	3	4	4	3	4	4	71
Round 3	4	4	4	4	4	3	4	5	5	4	3	4	3	5	4	3	5	6	74
Round 4	4	5	3	4	4	3	4	4	4	4	3	3	4	5	4	4	4	5	71	285
TOM KITE																			
Round 1	4	5	3	4	4	3	4	5	4	4	3	4	4	7	4	3	4	4	73
Round 2	4	4	3	5	4	3	4	5	4	4	2	4	4	6	4	3	5	5	73
Round 3	4	3	3	4	3	4	4	3	4	4	3	4	4	5	4	3	4	4	67
Round 4	4	4	2	4	4	2	4	4	4	6	3	4	5	5	4	3	5	5	72	285

RECORDS OF
THE OPEN CHAMPIONSHIP

Most victories
6, Harry Vardon, 1896–98–99–1903–11–14
5, James Braid, 1901–05–06–08–10; J.H. Taylor,
1894–95–1900–09–13; Peter Thomson, 1954–
55–56–58–65; Tom Watson, 1975–77–80–82–83

Most times runner-up or joint runner-up
7, Jack Nicklaus, 1964–67–68–72–76–77–79
6, J.H. Taylor, 1896–1904–05–06–07–14

Oldest winner
Old Tom Morris, 46 years 99 days, 1867
Roberto de Vicenzo, 44 years 93 days, 1967

Youngest winner
Young Tom Morris, 17 years 5 months 8 days, 1868
Willie Auchterlonie, 21 years 24 days, 1893
Severiano Ballesteros, 22 years 3 months 12 days, 1979

Youngest and oldest competitor
John Ball, 14 years, 1878
Gene Sarazen, 71 years 4 months 13 days, 1973

Biggest margin of victory
13 strokes, Old Tom Morris, 1862
12 strokes, Young Tom Morris, 1870
8 strokes, J.H. Taylor, 1900 and 1913; James
Braid, 1908
6 strokes, Bobby Jones, 1927; Walter Hagen, 1929;
Arnold Palmer, 1962; Johnny Miller, 1976

Lowest winning aggregates
268 (68, 70, 65, 65), Tom Watson, Turnberry, 1977
271 (68, 70, 64, 69), Tom Watson, Muirfield, 1980
275 (67, 68, 70, 70), Tom Watson, Royal Birkdale,
1983
276 (71, 69, 67, 69), Arnold Palmer, Troon, 1962
276 (68, 67, 71, 70), Tom Weiskopf, Troon, 1973
276 (72, 66, 67, 71), Bill Rogers, Sandwich, 1981
276 (69, 68, 70, 69), Severiano Ballesteros, St
Andrews, 1984

Lowest aggregates by runner-up
269 (68, 70, 65, 66), Jack Nicklaus, Turnberry, 1977
275 (68, 67, 71, 69), Lee Trevino, Muirfield, 1980

Lowest aggregate by an amateur
283 (74, 70, 71, 68), Guy Wolstenholme, St
Andrews, 1960

Lowest individual round
63, Mark Hayes, second round, Turnberry, 1977;
Isao Aoki, third round, Muirfield, 1980

Lowest individual round by an amateur
66, Frank Stranahan, fourth round, Troon, 1950

Lowest first round
64, Craig Stadler, Royal Birkdale, 1983
64, Christy O'Connor Jr, Royal St George's, 1985

Lowest second round
63, Mark Hayes, Turnberry, 1977

Lowest third round
63, Isao Aoki, Muirfield, 1980
64, Hubert Green and Tom Watson, Muirfield, 1980

Lowest fourth round
64, Graham Marsh, Royal Birkdale, 1983

Lowest first 36 holes
132 (67, 65), Henry Cotton, Sandwich, 1934
133 (67, 66), Bobby Clampett, Royal Troon, 1982

Lowest second 36 holes
130 (65, 65), Tom Watson, Turnberry, 1977

Lowest first 54 holes
202 (68, 70, 64), Tom Watson, Muirfield, 1980
203 (68, 70, 65), Jack Nicklaus and Tom Watson,
Turnberry, 1977

Lowest final 54 holes
200 (70, 65, 65), Tom Watson, Turnberry, 1977

Lowest 9 holes
28, Denis Durnian, first 9, Royal Birkdale, 1983
29, Peter Thomson and Tom Haliburton, first 9,
Royal Lytham, 1958; Tony Jacklin, first 9, St Andrews,
1970; Bill Longmuir, first 9, Royal Lytham, 1979

Winner in three decades
Gary Player, 1959, 1968, 1974

Biggest span between first and last victories
19 years, J.H. Taylor, 1894–1913
18 years, Harry Vardon, 1896–1914
15 years, Gary Player, 1959–74
14 years, Henry Cotton, 1934–48

Successive victories
4, Young Tom Morris, 1868–72. No championship
in 1871
3, Jamie Anderson, 1877–79; Bob Ferguson,
1880–82; Peter Thomson, 1954–56
2, Old Tom Morris, 1861–62; J.H. Taylor, 1894–95;
Harry Vardon, 1898–99; James Braid, 1905–06;
Bobby Jones, 1926–27; Walter Hagen, 1928–29;
Bobby Locke, 1949–50; Arnold Palmer, 1961–62;
Lee Trevino, 1971–72; Tom Watson, 1982–83

Victories by amateurs
3, Bobby Jones, 1926–27–30
2, Harold Hilton, 1892–97
1, John Ball, 1890
Roger Wethered lost a play-off in 1921

Highest number of top five finishes
16, J.H. Taylor and Jack Nicklaus
15, Harry Vardon and James Braid

Highest number of rounds under 70
28, Jack Nicklaus
16, Tom Watson, Lee Trevino
15, Peter Thomson
13, Gary Player
12, Bobby Locke, Arnold Palmer
11, Severiano Ballesteros

Outright leader after every round
Willie Auchterlonie, 1893; J.H. Taylor, 1894 and
1900; James Braid, 1908; Ted Ray, 1912; Bobby
Jones, 1927; Gene Sarazen, 1932; Henry Cotton,
1934; Tom Weiskopf, 1973

Lowest round in a play-off
67, Bobby Locke, Sandwich, 1949
68, Peter Thomson, Royal Lytham, 1958; Bobby Locke, Sandwich, 1949

Record leads (since 1892)
After 18 holes:
4 strokes, James Braid, 1908; Bobby Jones, 1927; Henry Cotton, 1934; Christy O'Connor Jr, 1985
After 36 holes:
9 strokes, Henry Cotton, 1934
After 54 holes:
10 strokes, Henry Cotton, 1934
 7 strokes, Tony Lema, 1964
 6 strokes, James Braid, 1908
 5 strokes, Arnold Palmer, 1962; Bill Rogers, 1981

Champions with each round lower than previous one
Jack White, 1904, Sandwich, 80, 75, 72, 69
James Braid, 1906, Muirfield, 77, 76, 74, 73
Ben Hogan, 1953, Carnoustie, 73, 71, 70, 68
Gary Player, 1959, Muirfield, 75, 71, 70, 68

Champion with four rounds the same
Densmore Shute, 1933, St Andrews, 73, 73, 73, 73 (excluding the play-off)

Biggest variation between rounds of a champion
14 strokes, Henry Cotton, 1934, second round 65, fourth round 79
11 strokes, Jack White, 1904, first round 80, fourth round 69

Biggest variation between two rounds
17 strokes, Jack Nicklaus, 1981, first round 83, second round 66

Best comeback by champions
After 18 holes:
Harry Vardon, 1896, 11 strokes behind the leader
After 36 holes:
George Duncan, 1920, 13 strokes behind the leader
After 54 holes:
Jim Barnes, 1925, 5 strokes behind the leader

Champions with four rounds under 70
None
Arnold Palmer, 1962, Tom Watson, 1977 and 1980, and Severiano Ballesteros, 1984, had three rounds under 70
Of non-champions, Phil Rodgers, 1963, Jack Nicklaus, 1977, Lee Trevino, 1980, and Nick Faldo, 1984, had three rounds under 70

Best finishing round by a champion
65, Tom Watson, Turnberry, 1977
66, Johnny Miller, Royal Birkdale, 1976

Worst finishing round by a champion since 1920
79, Henry Cotton, Sandwich, 1934
78, Reg Whitcombe, Sandwich, 1938
77, Walter Hagen, Hoylake, 1924

Worst opening round by a champion since 1919
80, George Duncan, Deal, 1920 (he also had a second round of 80)
77, Walter Hagen, Hoylake, 1924

Best opening round by a champion
66, Peter Thomson, Royal Lytham, 1958
67, Henry Cotton, Sandwich, 1934; Tom Watson, Royal Birkdale, 1983

Biggest recovery in 18 holes by a champion
George Duncan, Deal, 1920, was 13 strokes behind the leader, Abe Mitchell, after 36 holes and level after 54

Most appearances on final day (since 1892)
30, J.H. Taylor
27, Harry Vardon, James Braid
26, Peter Thomson
23, Dai Rees, Jack Nicklaus
22, Henry Cotton

Championship with highest number of rounds under 70
68, Royal Birkdale, 1983

Championship since 1946 with the fewest rounds under 70
St Andrews, 1946; Hoylake, 1947; Portrush, 1951; Hoylake, 1956; Carnoustie, 1968. All had only two rounds under 70

Longest course
Carnoustie, 1968, 7252 yd (6631 m)

Courses most often used
Prestwick, 24 (but not since 1925); St Andrews, 23; Muirfield, 12; Sandwich, 11; Hoylake, 10; Royal Lytham, 7; Musselburgh and Royal Birkdale, 6; Carnoustie, 5; Royal Troon, 5; Deal, 2; Royal Portrush, Prince's and Turnberry, 1

Prize Money

Year	Total	First Prize
1860	nil	nil
1863	10	nil
1864	16	6
1876	20	20
1889	22	8
1891	28.50	10
1892	110	(Amateur winner)
1893	100	30
1910	125	50
1920	225	75
1927	275	100
1930	400	100
1931	500	100
1946	1,000	150
1949	1,700	300
1953	2,450	500
1954	3,500	750
1955	3,750	1,000
1958	4,850	1,000
1959	5,000	1,000
1960	7,000	1,250
1961	8,500	1,400
1963	8,500	1,500
1965	10,000	1,750
1966	15,000	2,100
1968	20,000	3,000
1969	30,000	4,250
1970	40,000	5,250
1971	45,000	5,500
1972	50,000	5,500
1975	75,000	7,500
1977	100,000	10,000
1978	125,000	12,500
1979	155,000	15,500
1980	200,000	25,000
1981	200,000	25,000
1982	250,000	32,000
1983	300,000	40,000
1984	451,000	55,000
1985	530,000	65,000

Attendance

Year	Attendance
1962	37,098
1963	24,585
1964	35,954
1965	32,927
1966	40,182
1967	29,880
1968	51,819
1969	46,001
1970	81,593
1971	70,076
1972	84,746
1973	78,810
1974	92,796
1975	85,258
1976	92,021
1977	87,615
1978	125,271
1979	134,501
1980	131,610
1981	111,987
1982	133,299
1983	142,892
1984	193,126
1985	138,027

The largest single day attendance was 39,755 on the Saturday of the 1984 championship.

PAST RESULTS

★ Denotes amateurs

1860 Prestwick

Willie Park, Musselburgh	55	59	60	174
Tom Morris Sr, Prestwick	58	59	59	176
Andrew Strath, St Andrews				180
Robert Andrew, Perth				191
George Brown, Blackheath				192
Charles Hunter, Prestwick St Nicholas				195

1861 Prestwick

Tom Morris Sr, Prestwick	54	56	53	163
Willie Park, Musselburgh	54	54	59	167
William Dow, Musselburgh	59	58	54	171
David Park, Musselburgh	58	57	57	172
Robert Andrew, Perth	58	61	56	175
Peter McEwan, Bruntsfield	56	60	62	178

1862 Prestwick

Tom Morris Sr, Prestwick	52	55	56	163
Willie Park, Musselburgh	59	59	58	176
Charles Hunter, Prestwick	60	60	58	178
William Dow, Musselburgh	60	58	63	181
★ James Knight, Prestwick	62	61	63	186
★ J.F. Johnston, Prestwick	64	69	75	208

1863 Prestwick

Willie Park, Musselburgh	56	54	58	168
Tom Morris Sr, Prestwick	56	58	56	170
David Park, Musselburgh	55	63	54	172
Andrew Strath, St Andrews	61	55	58	174
George Brown, St Andrews	58	61	57	176
Robert Andrew, Perth	62	57	59	178

1864 Prestwick

Tom Morris Sr, Prestwick	54	58	55	167
Andrew Strath, St Andrews	56	57	56	169
Robert Andrew, Perth	57	58	60	175
Willie Park, Musselburgh	55	67	55	177
William Dow, Musselburgh	56	58	67	181
William Strath, St Andrews	60	62	60	182

1865 Prestwick

Andrew Strath, St Andrews	55	54	53	162
Willie Park, Musselburgh	56	52	56	164
William Dow, Musselburgh				171
Robert Kirk, St Andrews	64	54	55	173
Tom Morris Sr, St Andrews	57	61	56	174
★ William Doleman, Glasgow	62	57	59	178

1866 Prestwick

Willie Park, Musselburgh	54	56	59	169
David Park, Musselburgh	58	57	56	171
Robert Andrew, Perth	58	59	59	176
Tom Morris Sr, St Andrews	61	58	59	178
Robert Kirk, St Andrews	60	62	58	180
Andrew Strath, Prestwick	61	61	60	182
★ William Doleman, Glasgow	60	60	62	182

1867 Prestwick

Tom Morris Sr, St Andrews	58	54	58	170
Willie Park, Musselburgh	58	56	58	172
Andrew Strath, St Andrews	61	57	56	174
Tom Morris Jr, St Andrews	58	59	58	175
Robert Kirk, St Andrews	57	60	60	177
★ William Doleman, Glasgow	55	66	57	178

1868 Prestwick

Tom Morris Jr, St Andrews	50	55	52	157
Robert Andrew, Perth	53	54	52	159
Willie Park, Musselburgh	58	50	54	162
Robert Kirk, St Andrews	56	59	56	171
John Allan, Westward Ho!	54	55	63	172
Tom Morris Sr, St Andrews	56	62	58	176

1869 Prestwick

Tom Morris Jr, St Andrews	51	54	49	154
Tom Morris Sr, St Andrews	54	50	53	157
★ S. Mure Fergusson, Royal and Ancient	57	54	54	165
Robert Kirk, St Andrews	53	58	57	168
David Strath, St Andrews	53	56	60	169
Jamie Anderson, St Andrews	60	56	57	173

1870 Prestwick

Tom Morris Jr, St Andrews	47	51	51	149
Bob Kirk, Royal Blackheath	52	52	57	161
David Strath, St Andrews	54	49	58	161
Tom Morris Sr, St Andrews	56	52	54	162
★ William Doleman, Musselburgh	57	56	58	171
Willie Park, Musselburgh	60	55	58	173

1871 No Competition

1872 Prestwick

Tom Morris Jr, St Andrews	57	56	53	166
David Strath, St Andrews	56	52	61	169
★ William Doleman, Musselburgh	63	60	54	177
Tom Morris Sr, St Andrews	62	60	57	179
David Park, Musselburgh	61	57	61	179
Charlie Hunter, Prestwick	60	60	69	189

1873 St Andrews

Tom Kidd, St Andrews	91	88	179
Jamie Anderson, St Andrews	91	89	180
Tom Morris Jr, St Andrews	94	89	183
Bob Kirk, Royal Blackheath	91	92	183
David Strath, St Andrews	97	90	187
Walter Gourlay, St Andrews	92	96	188

1874 Musselburgh

Mungo Park, Musselburgh	75	84	159
Tom Morris Jr, St Andrews	83	78	161
George Paxton, Musselburgh	80	82	162
Bob Martin, St Andrews	85	79	164
Jamie Anderson, St Andrews	82	83	165
David Park, Musselburgh	83	83	166
W. Thomson, Edinburgh	84	82	166

1875 Prestwick

Willie Park, Musselburgh	56	59	51	166
Bob Martin, St Andrews	56	58	54	168
Mungo Park, Musselburgh	59	57	55	171
Robert Ferguson, Musselburgh	58	56	58	172
James Rennie, St Andrews	61	59	57	177
David Strath, St Andrews	59	61	58	178

1876 St Andrews

Bob Martin, St Andrews	86	90	176
David Strath, North Berwick	86	90	176
(Martin was awarded the title when Strath refused to play-off)			
Willie Park, Musselburgh	94	89	183
Tom Morris Sr, St Andrews	90	95	185
W. Thomson, Elie	90	95	185
Mungo Park, Musselburgh	95	90	185

1877 Musselburgh

Jamie Anderson, St Andrews	40	42	37	41	160
Bob Pringle, Musselburgh	44	38	40	40	162
Bob Ferguson, Musselburgh	40	40	40	44	164
William Cosgrove, Musselburgh	41	39	44	40	164
David Strath, North Berwick	45	40	38	43	166
William Brown, Musselburgh	39	41	45	41	166

1878 Prestwick

Jamie Anderson, St Andrews	53	53	51	157
Bob Kirk, St Andrews	53	55	51	159
J.O.F. Morris, St Andrews	50	56	55	161
Bob Martin, St Andrews	57	53	55	165
★ John Ball, Hoylake	53	57	55	165
Willie Park, Musselburgh	53	56	57	166
William Cosgrove, Musselburgh	55	56	55	166

1879 St Andrews

Jamie Anderson, St Andrews	84	85	169
James Allan, Westward Ho!	88	84	172
Andrew Kirkaldy, St Andrews	86	86	172
George Paxton, Musselburgh			174
Tom Kidd, St Andrews			175
Bob Ferguson, Musselburgh			176

1880 Musselburgh

Bob Ferguson, Musselburgh	81	81	162
Peter Paxton, Musselburgh	81	86	167
Ned Cosgrove, Musselburgh	82	86	168
George Paxton, Musselburgh	85	84	169
Bob Pringle, Musselburgh	90	79	169
David Brown, Musselburgh	86	83	169

1881 Prestwick

Bob Ferguson, Musselburgh	53	60	57	170
Jamie Anderson, St Andrews	57	60	56	173
Ned Cosgrove, Musselburgh	61	59	57	177
Bob Martin, St Andrews	57	62	59	178
Tom Morris Sr, St Andrews	58	65	58	181
Willie Campbell, Musselburgh	60	56	65	181
Willie Park Jr, Musselburgh	66	57	58	181

1882 St Andrews

Bob Ferguson, Musselburgh	83	88	171
Willie Fernie, Dumfries	88	86	174
Jamie Anderson, St Andrews	87	88	175
John Kirkaldy, St Andrews	86	89	175
Bob Martin, St Andrews	89	86	175
★ Fitz Boothby, St Andrews	86	89	175

1883 Musselburgh

Willie Fernie, Dumfries	75	84	159
Bob Ferguson, Musselburgh	78	80	159
(Fernie won play-off 158 to 159)			
William Brown, Musselburgh	83	77	160
Bob Pringle, Musselburgh	79	82	161
Willie Campbell, Musselburgh	80	83	163
George Paxton, Musselburgh	80	83	163

1884 Prestwick

Jack Simpson, Carnoustie	78	82	160
David Rollan, Elie	81	83	164
Willie Fernie, Felixstowe	80	84	164
Willie Campbell, Musselburgh	84	85	169
Willie Park Jr, Musselburgh	86	83	169
Ben Sayers, North Berwick	83	87	170

1885 St Andrews

Bob Martin, St Andrews	84	87	171
Archie Simpson, Carnoustie	83	89	172
David Ayton, St Andrews	89	84	173
Willie Fernie, Felixstowe	89	85	174
Willie Park Jr, Musselburgh	86	88	174
Bob Simpson, Carnoustie	85	89	174

1886 Musselburgh

David Brown, Musselburgh	79	78	157
Willie Campbell, Musselburgh	78	81	159
Ben Campbell, Musselburgh	79	81	160
Archie Simpson, Carnoustie	82	79	161
Willie Park Jr, Musselburgh	84	77	161
Thomas Gossett, Musselburgh	82	79	161
Bob Ferguson, Musselburgh	82	79	161

1887 Prestwick

Willie Park Jr, Musselburgh	82	79	161
Bob Martin, St Andrews	81	81	162
Willie Campbell, Prestwick	77	87	164
★ Johnny Laidlay, Honourable Company	86	80	166
Ben Sayers, North Berwick	83	85	168
Archie Simpson, Carnoustie	81	87	168

1888 St Andrews

Jack Burns, Warwick	86	85	171
David Anderson Jr, St Andrews	86	86	172
Ben Sayers, North Berwick	85	87	172
Willie Campbell, Prestwick	84	90	174
★ Leslie Balfour, Edinburgh	86	89	175
Andrew Kirkaldy, St Andrews	87	89	176
David Grant, North Berwick	88	88	176

1889 Musselburgh

Willie Park Jr, Musselburgh	39	39	39	38	155
Andrew Kirkaldy, St Andrews	39	38	39	39	155
(Park won play-off 158 to 163)					
Ben Sayers, North Berwick	39	40	41	39	159
★ Johnny Laidlay, Honourable Company	42	39	40	41	162
David Brown, Musselburgh	43	39	41	39	162
Willie Fernie, Troon	45	39	40	40	164

1890 Prestwick

★ John Ball, Royal Liverpool		82	82	164
Willie Fernie, Troon		85	82	167
Archie Simpson, Carnoustie		85	82	167
Willie Park Jr, Musselburgh		90	80	170
Andrew Kirkaldy, St Andrews		81	89	170
★ Horace Hutchinson, Royal North Devon		87	85	172

1891 St Andrews

Hugh Kirkaldy, St Andrews		83	83	166
Willie Fernie, Troon		84	84	168
Andrew Kirkaldy, St Andrews		84	84	168
S. Mure Fergusson, Royal and Ancient		86	84	170
W. D. More, Chester		84	87	171
Willie Park Jr, Musselburgh		88	85	173

(From 1892 the competition was extended to 72 holes)

1892 Muirfield

★ Harold Hilton, Royal Liverpool	78	81	72	74	305
★ John Ball Jr, Royal Liverpool	75	80	74	79	308
James Kirkaldy, St Andrews	77	83	73	75	308
Sandy Herd, Huddersfield	77	78	77	76	308
J. Kay, Seaton Carew	82	78	74	78	312
Ben Sayers, North Berwick	80	76	81	75	312

1893 Prestwick

Willie Auchterlonie, St Andrews	78	81	81	82	322
★ Johnny Laidlay, Honourable Company	80	83	80	81	324
Sandy Herd, Huddersfield	82	81	78	84	325
Hugh Kirkaldy, St Andrews	83	79	82	82	326
Andrew Kirkaldy, St Andrews	85	82	82	77	326
J. Kay, Seaton Carew	81	81	80	85	327
R. Simpson, Carnoustie	81	81	80	85	327

1894 Sandwich

J.H. Taylor, Winchester	84	80	81	81	326
Douglas Rolland, Limpsfield	86	79	84	82	331
Andrew Kirkaldy, St Andrews	86	79	83	84	332
A. Toogood, Eltham	84	85	82	82	333
Willie Fernie, Troon	84	84	86	80	334
Harry Vardon, Bury St Edmunds	86	86	82	80	334
Ben Sayers, North Berwick	85	81	84	84	334

1895 St Andrews

J.H. Taylor, Winchester	86	78	80	78	322
Sandy Herd, Huddersfield	82	77	82	85	326
Andrew Kirkaldy, St Andrews	81	83	84	84	332
G. Pulford, Royal Liverpool	84	81	83	87	335
Archie Simpson, Aberdeen	88	85	78	85	336
Willie Fernie, Troon	86	79	86	86	337
David Brown, Malvern	81	89	83	84	337
David Anderson, Panmure	86	83	84	84	337

1896 Muirfield

Harry Vardon, Ganton	83	78	78	77	316
J.H. Taylor, Winchester	77	78	81	80	316
(Vardon won play-off 157 to 161)					
★ Freddie G. Tait, Black Watch	83	75	84	77	319
Willie Fernie, Troon	78	79	82	80	319
Sandy Herd, Huddersfield	72	84	79	85	320
James Braid, Romford	83	81	79	80	323

1897 Hoylake

★ Harold H. Hilton, Royal Liverpool	80	75	84	75	314
James Braid, Romford	80	74	82	79	315
★ Freddie G. Tait, Black Watch	79	79	80	79	317
G. Pulford, Royal Liverpool	80	79	79	79	317
Sandy Herd, Huddersfield	78	81	79	80	318
Harry Vardon, Ganton	84	80	80	76	320

1898 Prestwick

Harry Vardon, Ganton	79	75	77	76	307
Willie Park, Musselburgh	76	75	78	79	308
★ Harold H. Hilton, Royal Liverpool	76	81	77	75	309
J.H. Taylor, Winchester	78	78	77	79	312
★ Freddie G. Tait, Black Watch	81	77	75	82	315
D. Kinnell, Leven	80	77	79	80	316

1899 Sandwich

Harry Vardon, Ganton	76	76	81	77	310
Jack White, Seaford	79	79	82	75	315
Andrew Kirkaldy, St Andrews	81	79	82	77	319
J.H. Taylor, Mid-Surrey	77	76	83	84	320
James Braid, Romford	78	78	83	84	322
Willie Fernie, Troon	79	83	82	78	322

1900 St Andrews

J.H. Taylor, Mid-Surrey	79	77	78	75	309
Harry Vardon, Ganton	79	81	80	78	317
James Braid, Romford	82	81	80	79	322
Jack White, Seaford	80	81	82	80	323
Willie Auchterlonie, St Andrews	81	85	80	80	326
Willie Park Jr, Musselburgh	80	83	81	84	328

1901 Muirfield

James Braid, Romford	79	76	74	80	309
Harry Vardon, Ganton	77	78	79	78	312
J.H. Taylor, Mid-Surrey	79	83	74	77	313
Harold H. Hilton, Royal Liverpool	89	80	75	76	320
Sandy Herd, Huddersfield	87	81	81	76	325
Jack White, Seaford	82	82	80	82	326

1902 Hoylake

Sandy Herd, Huddersfield	77	76	73	81	307
Harry Vardon, South Herts	72	77	80	79	308
James Braid, Walton Heath	78	76	80	74	308
R. Maxwell, Honourable Company	79	77	79	74	309
Tom Vardon, Ilkley	80	76	78	79	313
J.H. Taylor, Mid-Surrey	81	76	77	80	314
D. Kinnell, Leven	78	80	79	77	314
★ Harold Hilton, Royal Liverpool	79	76	81	78	314

1903 Prestwick

Harry Vardon, South Herts	73	77	72	78	300
Tom Vardon, Ilkley	76	81	75	74	306
Jack White, Sunningdale	77	78	74	79	308
Sandy Herd, Huddersfield	73	83	76	77	309
James Braid, Walton Heath	77	79	79	75	310
R. Thompson, North Berwick	83	78	77	76	314
A.H. Scott, Elie	77	77	83	77	314

1904 Sandwich

Jack White, Sunningdale	80	75	72	69	296
James Braid, Walton Heath	77	80	69	71	297
J.H. Taylor, Mid-Surrey	77	78	74	68	297
Tom Vardon, Ilkley	77	77	75	72	301
Harry Vardon, South Herts	76	73	79	74	302
James Sherlock, Stoke Poges	83	71	78	77	309

1905 St Andrews

James Braid, Walton Heath	81	78	78	81	318
J.H. Taylor, Mid-Surrey	80	85	78	80	323
R. Jones, Wimbledon	81	77	87	78	323
J. Kinnell, Purley Downs	82	79	82	81	324
Arnaud Massy, La Boulie	81	80	82	82	325
E. Gray, Littlehampton	82	81	84	78	325

1906 Muirfield

James Braid, Walton Heath	77	76	74	73	300
J.H. Taylor, Mid-Surrey	77	72	75	80	304
Harry Vardon, South Herts	77	73	77	78	305
J. Graham Jr, Royal Liverpool	71	79	78	78	306
R. Jones, Wimbledon Park	74	78	73	83	308
Arnaud Massy, La Boulie	76	80	76	78	310

1907 Hoylake

Arnaud Massy, La Boulie	76	81	78	77	312
J.H. Taylor, Mid-Surrey	79	79	76	80	314
Tom Vardon, Sandwich	81	81	80	75	317
G. Pulford, Royal Liverpool	81	78	80	78	317
Ted Ray, Ganton	83	80	79	76	318
James Braid, Walton Heath	82	85	75	76	318

1908 Prestwick

James Braid, Walton Heath	70	72	77	72	291
Tom Ball, West Lancashire	76	73	76	74	299
Ted Ray, Ganton	79	71	75	76	301
Sandy Herd, Huddersfield	74	74	79	75	302
Harry Vardon, South Herts	79	78	74	75	306
D. Kinnell, Prestwick St Nicholas	75	73	80	78	306

1909 Deal

J.H. Taylor, Mid-Surrey	74	73	74	74	295
James Braid, Walton Heath	79	73	73	74	299
Tom Ball, West Lancashire	74	75	76	76	301
C. Johns, Southdown	72	76	79	75	302
T.G. Renouf, Manchester	76	78	76	73	303
Ted Ray, Ganton	77	76	76	75	304

1910 St Andrews

James Braid, Walton Heath	76	73	74	76	299
Sandy Herd, Huddersfield	78	74	75	76	303
George Duncan, Hanger Hill	73	77	71	83	304
Laurie Ayton, Bishops Stortford	78	76	75	77	306
Ted Ray, Ganton	76	77	74	81	308
W. Smith, Mexico	77	71	80	80	308
J. Robson, West Surrey	75	80	77	76	308

1911 Sandwich

Harry Vardon, South Herts	74	74	75	80	303
Arnaud Massy, St Jean de Luz	75	78	74	76	303
(Play-off; Massy conceded at the 35th hole)					
Harold Hilton, Royal Liverpool	76	74	78	76	304
Sandy Herd, Coombe Hill	77	73	76	78	304
Ted Ray, Ganton	76	72	79	78	305
James Braid, Walton Heath	78	75	74	78	305
J.H. Taylor, Mid-Surrey	72	76	78	79	305

1912 Muirfield

Ted Ray, Oxhey	71	73	76	75	295
Harry Vardon, South Herts	75	72	81	71	299
James Braid, Walton Heath	77	71	77	78	303
George Duncan, Hanger Hill	72	77	78	78	305
Laurie Ayton, Bishops Stortford	74	80	75	79	308
Sandy Herd, Coombe Hill	76	81	76	76	309

1913 Hoylake

J.H. Taylor, Mid-Surrey	73	75	77	79	304
Ted Ray, Oxhey	73	74	81	84	312
Harry Vardon, South Herts	79	75	79	80	313
M. Moran, Dollymount	76	74	89	74	313
Johnny J. McDermott, USA	75	80	77	83	315
T. G. Renouf, Manchester	75	78	84	78	315

1914 Prestwick

Harry Vardon, South Herts	73	77	78	78	306
J.H. Taylor, Mid-Surrey	74	78	74	83	309
H.B. Simpson, St Annes Old	77	80	78	75	310
Abe Mitchell, Sonning	76	78	79	79	312
Tom Williamson, Notts	75	79	79	79	312
R.G. Wilson, Croham Hurst	76	77	80	80	313

1920 Deal

George Duncan, Hanger Hill	80	80	71	72	303
Sandy Herd, Coombe Hill	72	81	77	75	305
Ted Ray, Oxhey	72	83	78	73	306
Abe Mitchell, North Foreland	74	73	84	76	307
Len Holland, Northampton	80	78	71	79	308
Jim Barnes, USA	79	74	77	79	309

1921 St Andrews

Jock Hutchison, USA	72	75	79	70	296
★ Roger Wethered, Royal and Ancient	78	75	72	71	296
(Hutchison won play-off 150 to 159)					
T. Kerrigan, USA	74	80	72	72	298
Arthur G. Havers, West Lancs	76	74	77	72	299
George Duncan, Hanger Hill	74	75	78	74	301

1922 Sandwich

Walter Hagen, USA	76	73	79	72	300
George Duncan, Hanger Hill	76	75	81	69	301
Jim Barnes, USA	75	76	77	73	301
Jock Hutchison, USA	79	74	73	76	302
Charles Whitcombe, Dorchester	77	79	72	75	303
J.H. Taylor, Mid-Surrey	73	78	76	77	304

1923 Troon

Arthur G. Havers, Coombe Hill	73	73	73	76	295
Walter Hagen, USA	76	71	74	75	296
Macdonald Smith, USA	80	73	69	75	297
Joe Kirkwood, Australia	72	79	69	78	298
Tom Fernie, Turnberry	73	78	74	75	300
George Duncan, Hanger Hill	79	75	74	74	302
Charles A. Whitcombe, Landsdowne	70	76	74	82	302

1924 Hoylake

Walter Hagen, USA	77	73	74	77	301
Ernest Whitcombe, Came Down	77	70	77	78	302
Macdonald Smith, USA	76	74	77	77	304
F. Ball, Langley Park	78	75	74	77	304
J.H. Taylor, Mid-Surrey	75	74	79	79	307
George Duncan, Hanger Hill	74	79	74	81	308
Aubrey Boomer, St Cloud, Paris	75	78	76	79	308

1925 Prestwick

Jim Barnes, USA	70	77	79	74	300
Archie Compston, North Manchester	76	75	75	75	301
Ted Ray, Oxhey	77	76	75	73	301
Macdonald Smith, USA	76	69	76	82	303
Abe Mitchell, Unattached	77	76	75	77	305

1926 Royal Lytham

★ Robert T. Jones Jr, USA	72	72	73	74	291
Al Watrous, USA	71	75	69	78	293
Walter Hagen, USA	68	77	74	76	295
George von Elm, USA	75	72	76	72	295
Abe Mitchell, Unattached	78	78	72	71	299
T. Barber, Cavendish	77	73	78	71	299

1927 St Andrews

★ Robert T. Jones Jr, USA	68	72	73	72	285
Aubrey Boomer, St Cloud, Paris	76	70	73	72	291
Fred Robson, Cooden Beach	76	72	69	74	291
Joe Kirkwood, Australia	72	72	75	74	293
Ernest Whitcombe, Bournemouth	74	73	73	73	293
Charles Whitcombe, Crews Hill	74	76	71	75	296

1928 Sandwich

Walter Hagen, USA	75	73	72	72	292
Gene Sarazen, USA	72	76	73	73	294
Archie Compston, Unattached	75	74	73	73	295
Percy Alliss, Berlin	75	76	75	72	298
Fred Robson, Cooden Beach	79	73	73	73	298
Jose Jurado, Argentina	74	71	76	80	301
Aubrey Boomer, St Cloud, Paris	79	73	77	72	301
Jim Barnes, USA	81	73	76	71	301

1929 Muirfield

Walter Hagen, USA	75	67	75	75	292
John Farrell, USA	72	75	76	75	298
Leo Diegel, USA	71	69	82	77	299
Abe Mitchell, St Albans	72	72	78	78	300
Percy Alliss, Berlin	69	76	76	79	300
Bobby Cruickshank, USA	73	74	78	76	301

1930 Hoylake

★ Robert T. Jones Jr, USA	70	72	74	75	291
Leo Diegel, USA	74	73	71	75	293
Macdonald Smith, USA	70	77	75	71	293
Fred Robson, Cooden Beach	71	72	78	75	296
Horton Smith, USA	72	73	78	73	296
Archie Compston, Coombe Hill	74	73	68	82	297
Jim Barnes, USA	71	77	72	77	297

1931 Carnoustie

Tommy Armour, USA	73	75	77	71	296
Jose Jurado, Argentina	76	71	73	77	297
Percy Alliss, Berlin	74	78	73	73	298
Gene Sarazen, USA	74	76	75	73	298
Macdonald Smith, USA	75	77	71	76	299
John Farrell, USA	72	77	75	75	299

1932 Prince's

Gene Sarazen, USA	70	69	70	74	283
Macdonald Smith, USA	71	76	71	70	288
Arthur G. Havers, Sandy Lodge	74	71	68	76	289
Charles Whitcombe, Crews Hill	71	73	73	75	292
Percy Alliss, Beaconsfield	71	71	78	72	292
Alf Padgham, Royal Ashdown Forest	76	72	74	70	292

1933 St Andrews

Densmore Shute, USA	73	73	73	73	292
Craig Wood, USA	77	72	68	75	292
(Shute won play-off 149 to 154)					
Sid Easterbrook, Knowle	73	72	71	77	293
Gene Sarazen, USA	72	73	73	75	293
Leo Diegel, USA	75	70	71	77	293
Olin Dutra, USA	76	76	70	72	294

1934 Sandwich

Henry Cotton, Waterloo, Belgium	67	65	72	79	283
Sid Brews, South Africa	76	71	70	71	288
Alf Padgham, Sundridge Park	71	70	75	74	290
Macdonald Smith, USA	77	71	72	72	292
Joe Kirkwood, USA	74	69	71	78	292
Marcel Dallemagne, France	71	73	71	77	292

1935 Muirfield

Alf Perry, Leatherhead	69	75	67	72	283
Alf Padgham, Sundridge Park	70	72	74	71	287
Charles Whitcombe, Crews Hill	71	68	73	76	288
Bert Gadd, Brand Hall	72	75	71	71	289
Lawson Little, USA	75	71	74	69	289
Henry Picard, USA	72	73	72	75	292

1936 Hoylake

Alf Padgham, Sundridge Park	73	72	71	71	287
Jimmy Adams, Romford	71	73	71	73	288
Henry Cotton, Waterloo, Belgium	73	72	70	74	289
Marcel Dallemagne, France	73	72	75	69	289
Percy Alliss, Leeds Municipal	74	72	74	71	291
T. Green, Burnham Beeches	74	72	70	75	291
Gene Sarazen, USA	73	75	70	73	291

1937 Carnoustie

Henry Cotton, Ashridge	74	72	73	71	290
Reg Whitcombe, Parkstone	72	70	74	76	292
Charles Lacey, USA	76	75	70	72	293
Charles Whitcombe, Crews Hill	73	71	74	76	294
Bryon Nelson, USA	75	76	71	74	296
Ed Dudley, USA	70	74	78	75	297

1938 Sandwich

Reg Whitcombe, Parkstone	71	71	75	78	295
Jimmy Adams, Royal Liverpool	70	71	78	78	297
Henry Cotton, Ashridge	74	73	77	74	298
Alf Padgham, Sundridge Park	74	72	75	82	303
Jack Busson, Pannal	71	69	83	80	303
Richard Burton, Sale	71	69	78	85	303
Allan Dailey, Wanstead	73	72	80	78	303

1939 St Andrews

Richard Burton, Sale	70	72	77	71	290
Johnny Bulla, USA	77	71	71	73	292
Johnny Fallon, Huddersfield	71	73	71	79	294
Bill Shankland, Temple Newsam	72	73	72	77	294
Alf Perry, Leatherhead	71	74	73	76	294
Reg Whitcombe, Parkstone	71	75	74	74	294
Sam King, Knole Park	74	72	75	73	294

1946 St Andrews

Sam Snead, USA	71	70	74	75	290
Bobby Locke, South Africa	69	74	75	76	294
Johnny Bulla, USA	71	72	72	79	294
Charlie Ward, Little Aston	73	73	73	76	295
Henry Cotton, Royal Mid-Surrey	70	70	76	79	295
Dai Rees, Hindhead	75	67	73	80	295
Norman von Nida, Australia	70	76	74	75	295

1947 Hoylake

Fred Daly, Balmoral, Belfast	73	70	78	72	293
Reg Horne, Hendon	77	74	72	71	294
★ Frank Stranahan, USA	71	79	72	72	294
Bill Shankland, Temple Newsam	76	74	75	70	295
Richard Burton, Coombe Hill	77	71	77	71	296
Charlie Ward, Little Aston	76	73	76	72	297
Sam King, Wildernesse	75	72	77	73	297
Arthur Lees, Dore and Totley	75	74	72	76	297
Johnny Bulla, USA	80	72	74	71	297
Henry Cotton, Royal Mid-Surrey	69	78	74	76	297
Norman von Nida, Australia	74	76	71	76	297

1948 Muirfield

Henry Cotton, Royal Mid-Surrey	71	66	75	72	284
Fred Daly, Balmoral, Belfast	72	71	73	73	289
Norman von Nida, Australia	71	72	76	71	290
Roberto de Vicenzo, Argentina	70	73	72	75	290
Jack Hargreaves, Sutton Coldfield	76	68	73	73	290
Charlie Ward, Little Aston	69	72	75	74	290

1949 Sandwich

Bobby Locke, South Africa	69	76	68	70	283
Harry Bradshaw, Kilcroney, Eire	68	77	68	70	283
(Locke won play-off 135 to 147)					
Roberto de Vicenzo, Argentina	68	75	73	69	285
Sam King, Knole Park	71	69	74	72	286
Charlie Ward, Little Aston	73	71	70	72	286
Arthur Lees, Dore and Totley	74	70	72	71	287
Max Faulkner, Royal Mid-Surrey	71	71	71	74	287

1950 Troon

Bobby Locke, South Africa	69	72	70	68	279
Roberto de Vicenzo, Argentina	72	71	68	70	281
Fred Daly, Balmoral, Belfast	75	72	69	66	282
Dai Rees, South Herts	71	68	72	71	282
E. Moore, South Africa	74	68	73	68	283
Max Faulkner, Royal Mid-Surrey	73	70	70	71	283

1951 Royal Portrush

Max Faulkner, Unattached	71	70	70	74	285
Tony Cerda, Argentina	74	72	71	70	287
Charlie Ward, Little Aston	75	73	74	68	290
Fred Daly, Balmoral, Belfast	74	70	75	73	292
Jimmy Adams, Wentworth	68	77	75	72	292
Bobby Locke, South Africa	71	74	74	74	293
Bill Shankland, Temple Newsam	73	76	72	72	293
Norman Sutton, Leigh	73	70	74	76	293
Harry Weetman, Croham Hurst	73	71	75	74	293
Peter Thomson, Australia	70	75	73	75	293

1952 Royal Lytham

Bobby Locke, South Africa	69	71	74	73	287
Peter Thomson, Australia	68	73	77	70	288
Fred Daly, Balmoral, Belfast	67	69	77	76	289
Henry Cotton, Royal Mid-Surrey	75	74	74	71	294
Tony Cerda, Argentina	73	73	76	73	295
Sam King, Knole Park	71	74	74	76	295

1953 Carnoustie

Ben Hogan, USA	73	71	70	68	282
★ Frank Stranahan, USA	70	74	73	69	286
Dai Rees, South Herts	72	70	73	71	286
Peter Thomson, Australia	72	72	71	71	286
Tony Cerda, Argentina	75	71	69	71	286
Roberto de Vicenzo, Argentina	72	71	71	73	287

1954 Royal Birkdale

Peter Thomson, Australia	72	71	69	71	283
Sid Scott, Carlisle City	76	67	69	72	284
Dai Rees, South Herts	72	71	69	72	284
Bobby Locke, South Africa	74	71	69	70	284
Jimmy Adams, Royal Mid-Surrey	73	75	69	69	286
Tony Cerda, Argentina	71	71	73	71	286
J. Turnesa, USA	72	72	71	71	286

1955 St Andrews

Peter Thomson, Australia	71	68	70	72	281
Johnny Fallon, Huddersfield	73	67	73	70	283
Frank Jowle, Edgbaston	70	71	69	74	284
Bobby Locke, South Africa	74	69	70	72	285
Tony Cerda, Argentina	73	71	71	71	286
Ken Bousfield, Coombe Hill	71	75	70	70	286
Harry Weetman, Croham Hurst	71	71	70	74	286
Bernard Hunt, Hartsbourne	70	71	74	71	286
Flory van Donck, Belgium	71	72	71	72	286

1956 Hoylake

Peter Thomson, Australia	70	70	72	74	286
Flory van Donck, Belgium	71	74	70	74	289
Roberto de Vicenzo, Argentina	71	70	79	70	290
Gary Player, South Africa	71	76	73	71	291
John Panton, Glenbervie	74	76	72	70	292
Henry Cotton, Temple	72	76	71	74	293
E. Bertolino, Argentina	69	72	76	76	293

1957 St Andrews

Bobby Locke, South Africa	69	72	68	70	279
Peter Thomson, Australia	73	69	70	70	282
Eric Brown, Buchanan Castle	67	72	73	71	283
Angel Miguel, Spain	72	72	69	72	285
David Thomas, Sudbury	72	74	70	70	286
Tom Haliburton, Wentworth	72	73	68	73	286
★ Dick Smith, Prestwick	71	72	72	71	286
Flory van Donck, Belgium	72	68	74	72	286

1958 Royal Lytham

Peter Thomson, Australia	66	72	67	73	278
David Thomson, Sudbury	70	68	69	71	278
(Thomson won play-off 139 to 143)					
Eric Brown, Buchanan Castle	73	70	65	71	279
Christy O'Connor, Killarney	67	68	73	71	279
Flory van Donck, Belgium	70	70	67	74	281
Leopoldo Ruiz, Argentina	71	65	72	73	281

1959 Muirfield

Gary Player, South Africa	75	71	70	68	284
Flory van Donck, Belgium	70	70	73	73	286
Fred Bullock, Prestwick St Ninians	68	70	74	74	286
Sid Scott, Roehampton	73	70	73	71	287
Christy O'Connor, Royal Dublin	73	74	72	69	288
★ Reid Jack, Dullatur	71	75	68	74	288
Sam King, Knole Park	70	74	68	76	288
John Panton, Glenbervie	72	72	71	73	288

1960 St Andrews

Kel Nagle, Australia	69	67	71	71	278
Arnold Palmer, USA	70	71	70	68	279
Bernard Hunt, Hartsbourne	72	73	71	66	282
Harold Henning, South Africa	72	72	69	69	282
Robert de Vicenzo, Argentina	67	67	75	73	282
★ Guy Wolstenholme, Sunningdale	74	70	71	68	283

1961 Royal Birkdale

Arnold Palmer, USA	70	73	69	72	284
Dai Rees, South Herts	68	74	71	72	285
Christy O'Connor, Royal Dublin	71	77	67	73	288
Neil Coles, Coombe Hill	70	77	69	72	288
Eric Brown, Unattached	73	76	70	70	289
Kel Nagle, Australia	68	75	75	71	289

1962 Troon

Arnold Palmer, USA	71	69	67	69	276
Kel Nagle, Australia	71	71	70	70	282
Brian Huggett, Romford	75	71	74	69	289
Phil Rodgers, USA	75	70	72	72	289
Bob Charles, NZ	75	70	70	75	290
Sam Snead, USA	76	73	72	71	292
Peter Thomson, Australia	70	77	75	70	292

1963 Royal Lytham

Bob Charles, NZ	68	72	66	71	277
Phil Rodgers, USA	67	68	73	69	277
(Charles won play-off 140 to 148)					
Jack Nicklaus, USA	71	67	70	70	278
Kel Nagle, Australia	69	70	73	71	283
Peter Thomson, Australia	67	69	71	78	285
Christy O'Connor, Royal Dublin	74	68	76	68	286

1964 St Andrews

Tony Lema, USA	73	68	68	70	279
Jack Nicklaus, USA	76	74	66	68	284
Roberto de Vicenzo, Argentina	76	72	70	67	285
Bernard Hunt, Hartsbourne	73	74	70	70	287
Bruce Devlin, Australia	72	72	73	73	290
Christy O'Connor, Royal Dublin	71	73	74	73	291
Harry Weetman, Selsdon Park	72	71	75	73	291

1965 Royal Birkdale

Peter Thomson, Australia	74	68	72	71	285
Christy O'Connor, Royal Dublin	69	73	74	71	287
Briann Huggett, Romford	73	68	76	70	287
Robert de Vicenzo, Argentina	74	69	73	72	288
Kel Nagle, Australia	74	70	73	72	289
Tony Lema, USA	68	72	75	74	289
Bernard Hunt, Hartsbourne	74	74	70	71	289

1966 Muirfield

Jack Nicklaus, USA	70	67	75	70	282
David Thomas, Dunham Forest	72	73	69	69	283
Doug Sanders, USA	71	70	72	70	283
Gary Player, South Africa	72	74	71	69	286
Bruce Devlin, Australia	73	69	74	70	286
Kel Nagle, Australia	72	68	76	70	286
Phil Rodgers, USA	74	66	70	76	286

1967 Hoylake

Robert de Vicenzo, Argentina	70	71	67	70	278
Jack Nicklaus, USA	71	69	71	69	280
Clive Clark, Sunningdale	70	73	69	72	284
Gary Player, South Africa	72	71	67	74	284
Tony Jacklin, Potters Bar	73	69	73	70	285
Sebastian Miguel, Spain	72	74	68	72	286
Harold Henning, South Africa	74	70	71	71	286

1968 Carnoustie

Gary Player, South Africa	74	71	71	73	289
Jack Nicklaus, USA	76	69	73	73	291
Bob Charles, NZ	72	72	71	76	291
Billy Casper, USA	72	68	74	78	292
Maurice Bembridge, Little Aston	71	75	73	74	293
Brian Barnes, Burnham & Berrow	70	74	80	71	295
Neil Coles, Coombe Hill	75	76	71	73	295
Gay Brewer, USA	74	73	72	76	295

1969 Royal Lytham

Tony Jacklin, Potters Bar	68	70	70	72	280
Bob Charles, NZ	66	69	75	72	282
Peter Thomson, Australia	71	70	70	72	283
Roberto de Vicenzo, Argentina	72	73	66	72	283
Christy O'Connor, Royal Dublin	71	65	74	74	284
Jack Nicklaus, USA	75	70	68	72	285
Davis Love Jr, USA	70	73	71	71	285

1970 St Andrews

Jack Nicklaus, USA	68	69	73	73	283
Doug Sanders, USA	68	71	71	73	283
(Nicklaus won play-off 72 to 73)					
Harold Henning, South Africa	67	72	73	73	285
Lee Trevino, USA	68	68	72	77	285
Tony Jacklin, Potters Bar	67	70	73	76	286
Neil Coles, Coombe Hill	65	74	72	76	287
Peter Oosterhuis, Dulwich and Sydenham	73	69	69	76	287

1971 Royal Birkdale

Lee Trevino, USA	69	70	69	70	278
Lu Liang Huan, Taiwan	70	70	69	70	279
Tony Jacklin, Potters Bar	69	70	70	71	280
Craig de Foy, Coombe Hill	72	72	68	69	281
Jack Nicklaus, USA	71	71	72	69	283
Charles Coody, USA	74	71	70	68	283

1972 Muirfield

Lee Trevino, USA	71	70	66	71	278
Jack Nicklaus, USA	70	72	71	66	279
Tony Jacklin, Potters Bar	69	72	67	72	280
Doug Sanders, USA	71	71	69	70	281
Brian Barnes, Fairway D R	71	72	69	71	283
Gary Player, South Africa	71	71	76	67	285

1973 Troon

Tom Weiskopf, USA	68	67	71	70	276
Neil Coles, Holiday Inns	71	72	70	66	279
Johnny Miller, USA	70	68	69	72	279
Jack Nicklaus, USA	69	70	76	65	280
Bert Yancey, USA	69	69	73	70	281
Peter Butler, Golf Domes	71	72	74	69	286

1974 Royal Lytham

Gary Player, South Africa	69	68	75	70	282
Peter Oosterhuis, Pacific Harbour	71	71	73	71	286
Jack Nicklaus, USA	74	72	70	71	287
Hubert Green, USA	71	74	72	71	288
Danny Edwards, USA	70	73	76	73	292
Lu Liang Huan, Taiwan	72	72	75	73	292

1975 Carnoustie

Tom Watson, USA	71	67	69	72	279
Jack Newton, Australia	69	71	65	74	279
(Watson won play-off 71 to 72)					
Bobby Cole, South Africa	72	66	66	76	280
Jack Nicklaus, USA	69	71	68	72	280
Johnny Miller, USA	71	69	66	74	280
Graham Marsh, Australia	72	67	71	71	281

1976 Royal Birkdale

Johnny Miller, USA	72	68	73	66	279
Jack Nicklaus, USA	74	70	72	69	285
Severiano Ballesteros, Spain	69	69	73	74	285
Raymond Floyd, USA	76	67	73	70	286
Mark James, Burghley Park	76	72	74	66	288
Hubert Green, USA	72	70	78	68	288
Christy O'Connor Jr, Shannon	69	73	75	71	288
Tom Kite, USA	70	74	73	71	288
Tommy Horton, Royal Jersey	74	69	72	73	288

1977 Turnberry

Tom Watson, USA	68	70	65	65	268
Jack Nicklaus, USA	68	70	65	66	269
Hubert Green, USA	72	66	74	67	279
Lee Trevino, USA	68	70	72	70	280
Ben Crenshaw, USA	71	69	66	75	281
George Burns, USA	70	70	72	69	281

1978 St Andrews

Jack Nicklaus, USA	71	72	69	69	281
Simon Owen, NZ	70	75	67	71	283
Ben Crenshaw, USA	70	69	73	71	283
Raymond Floyd, USA	69	75	71	68	283
Tom Kite, USA	72	69	72	70	283
Peter Oosterhuis, GB	72	70	69	73	284

1979 Royal Lytham

Severiano Ballesteros, Spain	73	65	75	70	283
Jack Nicklaus, USA	72	69	73	72	286
Ben Crenshaw, USA	72	71	72	71	286
Mark James, Burghley Park	76	69	69	73	287
Rodger Davis, Australia	75	70	70	73	288
Hale Irwin, USA	68	68	75	78	289

1980 Muirfield

Tom Watson, USA	68	70	64	69	271
Lee Trevino, USA	68	67	71	69	275
Ben Crenshaw, USA	70	70	68	69	277
Jack Nicklaus, USA	73	67	71	69	280
Carl Mason, Unattached	72	69	70	69	280

1981 Sandwich

Bill Rogers, USA	72	66	67	71	276
Bernhard Langer, Germany	73	67	70	70	280
Mark James, Otley	72	70	68	73	283
Raymond Floyd, USA	74	70	69	70	283
Sam Torrance, Caledonian Hotel	72	69	73	70	284
Bruce Leitzke, USA	76	69	71	69	285
Manuel Pinero, Spain	73	74	68	70	285

1982 Troon

Tom Watson, USA	69	71	74	70	284
Peter Oosterhuis, GB	74	67	74	70	285
Nick Price, South Africa	69	69	74	73	285
Nick Faldo, Glynwed Ltd	73	73	71	69	286
Des Smyth, EAL Tubes	70	69	74	73	286
Tom Purtzer, USA	76	66	75	69	286
Massy Kuramoto, Japan	71	73	71	71	286

1983 Royal Birkdale

Tom Watson, USA	67	68	70	70	275
Hale Irwin, USA	69	68	72	67	276
Andy Bean, USA	70	69	70	67	276
Graham Marsh, Australia	69	70	74	64	277
Lee Trevino, USA	69	66	73	70	278
Severiano Ballesteros, Spain	71	71	69	68	279
Harold Henning, South Africa	71	69	70	69	279

1984 St Andrews

Severiano Ballesteros, Spain	69	68	70	69	276
Bernhard Langer, Germany	71	68	68	71	278
Tom Watson, USA	71	68	66	73	278
Fred Couples, USA	70	69	74	68	281
Lanny Wadkins, USA	70	69	73	69	281
Greg Norman, Australia	67	74	74	67	282
Nick Faldo, Glynwed Int.	69	68	76	69	282

THE ROYAL
ST. GEORGE'S
GOLF CLUB
SANDWICH

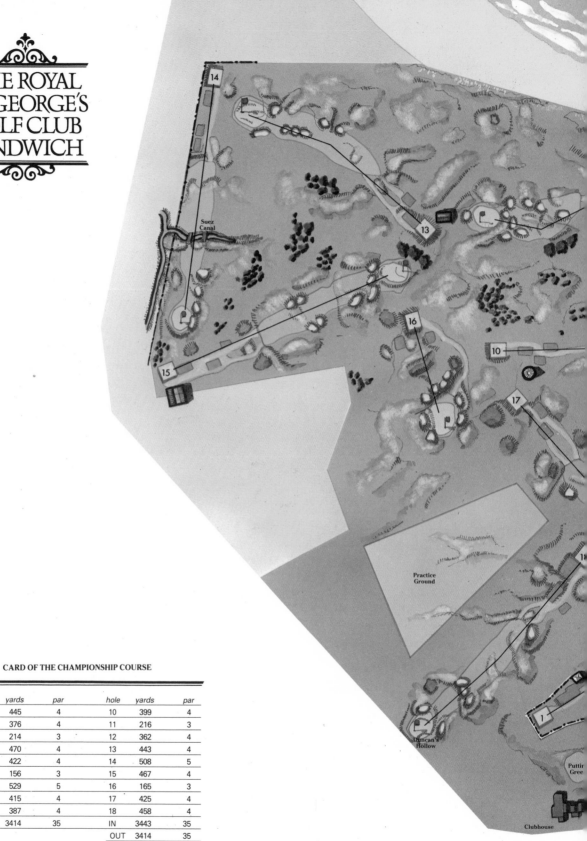

CARD OF THE CHAMPIONSHIP COURSE

hole	yards	par	hole	yards	par
1	445	4	10	399	4
2	376	4	11	216	3
3	214	3	12	362	4
4	470	4	13	443	4
5	422	4	14	508	5
6	156	3	15	467	4
7	529	5	16	165	3
8	415	4	17	425	4
9	387	4	18	458	4
OUT	3414	35	IN	3443	35
			OUT	3414	35
			TOTAL	6857	70